The Shipping Container Homes Book

A Shipping Container House Plans to Building an Environmentally Friendly Home, Plus Tips, and Design Ideas to Get You Started

By

Kenelm Hunt

Copyright © 2021 – Kenelm Hunt

All rights reserved

No part of this publication may be reproduced, distributed, or transmitted in any form or by any means, including photocopying, recording, or other electronic or mechanical methods, without the prior written permission of the publisher, except in the case of brief quotations embodied in reviews and certain other non-commercial uses permitted by copyright law.

Disclaimer

This publication is designed to provide competent and reliable information regarding the subject matter covered. However, the views expressed in this publication are those of the author alone, and should not be taken as expert instruction or professional advice. The reader is responsible for his or her own actions.

The author hereby disclaims any responsibility or liability whatsoever that is incurred from the use or application of the contents of this publication by the purchaser or reader. The purchaser or reader is hereby responsible for his or her own actions.

Table of Contents

Introduction 11

Chapter 1 13

Fundamentals of Shipping Container 13

    What is a Shipping Container? 13

    History of Shipping Container Homes 14

    Drawbacks of a Shipping Container Home 17

    Why Choose a Shipping Container Home? 21

Chapter 2 26

Tips To Know Before Starting The Process 26

Chapter 3 32

Planning Your Home Layout 32

    Plan 1: Empty Nester 32

    Plan 2: Happy Twogether 33

    Plan 3: Dwell Well 34

    Plan 4: Double Duo 35

Plan 5: Family Matters 2 Bedroom 36

Plan 6: Roommates 37

Chapter 4 38

Choosing The Right Container 38

Why is Container Condition Important? 38

When Should a Container be Inspected? 39

    Guidelines For Pre-purchase Inspection 39
    Guidelines For Post-Purchase Inspection 40

How and What to Inspect? 40

    Structural Frame 41
    Underside 41
    Walls 42
    Roof 43
    End Doors 43
    Interior 44
    Floor 44

Documentation 45

Conditions and Container Grades 47

    New (and New-ish) Containers 48
    One-Trip Containers 48
    Refurbished Containers 49
    Used Containers 49

Cargo Worthy (CW) Containers 50
As-Is Containers 50
Reasons to Choose New and (New-ish) Containers 51

Reasons to Choose Used Containers 52

Cost of Shipping Containers.. 54

The Condition of Shipping Container to Buy 55

Where to Buy Your Containers 57

    Online — In The US.. 58
    Online — Outside The US 59
    Finding Containers Offline 60
What To Lookout For When Choosing a Container Dealer
.... 61

    Integrity and Reputation... 61
    Warranties and Returns 63
    Volume Discounts.. 64
    Value-Added Services 65
    Delivery and Offloading 65

Chapter 5 67

Site Preparation and Foundation... 67

    Site Preparation 67

        Deciding on Location 67
        Sun and Shade 67

  Topography and Drainage 68
  Views.. 69
  Access... 69
 Site Work 69

  Marking and Staking 70
  Clearing and Grubbing 70
  Grading, Cut, and Fill.. 71
  Road Building.. 71
  Erosion Control 71
  Fencing and Security 72
 Foundation.. 72

  Is Foundation Required for Containers? 73
  Types of Foundations For Containers............................. 73
  Strength of Foundation Concrete to Use 77
  Attaching Containers to Foundations............................. 78
Chapter 6 78

Insulating The Container 78

 What is Insulation? 78

 Why Insulate Your Container?... 79

 Climatic Effects of Your Insulation Choice 80

 Placing Your Container Insulation 80

 What to Consider When Choosing Your Insulation 81

Types of Container Insulation 83

    Non-Traditional 83
    Blanket 84
    Loose-Fill 85
    Expanded Form 86
    Spray 88

Chapter 7 90

Receiving and Installing The Container 90

Distance-Based Delivery Charges 90

    Locally Sourced 90
    Internationally Sourced 91
Finding Companies to Ship Your Containers 93

Length of Time of Delivery 93

Siting and Offloading Your Shipping Containers 93

Chapter 8 96

Installing The Utilities 96

    Electricity 96

    Gas 97

    Sewer and Septic 97

    Telecommunications 97

    Water 98

Chapter 9 99

Roofing The Container 99

    Types of Roofing Styles 99

        Shed 100
        Gable 102
        Flat 104
    Why You Need a Structural Engineer? 105

Chapter 10 106

Flooring The Container 106

    Checking The Original Floors of The Container 106

    Should I Remove The Original Floor or Not? 106

        How to Remove The Original Floor? 107
        Replacing a Container Floor 107

        Best Flooring For Flatpack Containers 108

Chapter 11 109

Building A Wall Inside The Container 109

    Framing 109

    Insulation 111

Wall-Paneling 111

    Types of Container Interior Walls 112

Chapter 12 114

Installing The Doors and Windows 114

Chapter 13 120

Fixing The Exterior of The Container........................ 120

    Cladding Materials 120

        Timber... 121
        Bamboo... 122
        Engineered Wood 123
        Fiber-Cement Boards 124
        Composite Materials.. 125
        Composite Panels... 126
        Metal 127

    Cladding Installation 128

        Cladding Only 128
        Cladding With Exterior Insulation 129

    Painting The Container 129

Chapter 14 132

Interior Design Ideas 132

    Design Idea 1—Sliding doors............................. 132

- Barn Doors 133
- Pocket Doors 134
- Design Idea 2—Convertible Couches 134
  - Futon 135
  - Daybed 136
  - Foldout Couch/Sleeper Sofa Chaise 136
- Design Idea 3—Using The Walls 137
  - Wall-Mounted Desks 137
  - Tv Mounts 138
  - Wall-Mounted Fans 138
- Design Idea 4—Rooms Without Walls 139
  - Hanging Fabric Curtains 139
  - Hanging Beaded Curtains 139
  - Folding Panel Dividers 140
  - Rotating Entertainment Center 141
  - Double-Sided Fireplace 142

Chapter 15 143

Shipping Container Home FAQs 143

Chapter 16 153

Shipping Container Home Mistakes To Avoid 153

Conclusion 158

References 159

Introduction

Building an actual house can be very strenuous and expensive, and over the years, a solution was sought. There had to be a relatively cheaper house and easier to maintain than the usual ones available. For some other people, it was a chance to finally execute the brilliant ideas and designs that they had stacked up in their heads. So, something useful was discovered, and that is the cargo container used in transporting cargoes across the sea. The structure was just right for a house, and so, some very ingenious people thought about it being an actual house that people can live in.

So, gradually, with time, the shipping container home was implemented. It allows the chance of getting a house within a period of three months or less, depending on some factors that will be discussed later on in this book. This short time frame, as opposed to the years used in constructing the typical and traditional houses, was a big catch, and several people began to try it out. However, in as much as the concept of this sounds interesting, there usually are many things to consider.

Building a container home will require that you learn a couple of vital things so that you don't later have regrets. That is why this book, *The Shipping Container Homes Book*, was written. It contains several pricey information you will need in constructing your shipping container home from scratch, the do's and don'ts, and all you'd need is a measure of readiness.

So, let's begin proper, shall we?

Chapter 1

Fundamentals of Shipping Container

Shipping containers described here aren't the usual plastic containers you see around but are constructed from heavy and durable metallic components that give them an extremely sturdy and durable feature. In a bid to shed more light on these very sturdy metallic structures, we'd look at a few interesting sub-headings.

What is a Shipping Container?

Shipping containers are one of the very many ingenious productions of the world of architecture. They are containers whose functions have been re-engineered to be suitable for all kinds of projects with ties to construction. These containers can be constructed into small cubical cabins, mini-homes on wheels, much bigger homes, and several other compartment peculiarities.

Surprisingly, the art of making beautiful and homey structures out of containers has become a very wide field with its own intricacies and peculiarities. For instance, you could see some shipping containers with the medieval touch, the modern touch, or a fuse of the two. Some other containers are constructed so that the interiors are padded with actual walls that give the impression of actual concrete buildings.

History of Shipping Container Homes

Shipping containers were created for one sole reason. There was a need to transport goods across water bodies over the years. Man devised a whole lot of methods for this particular reason, but because of the inefficacies attached to each invention, there usually was another idea almost immediately. A few of the inefficacies include the following;

- The transportation of goods between countries was very slow and complicated.
- It required a whole lot of manpower and labor. Then, the goods were usually moved first from the warehouse to the dock, and then, they'd be loaded into crates or barrels. After barrels were loaded, they'd be manually carried into the ships. This process was regarded as the break-bulk process.
- There were several incidences of a hold-up at ports.

- The other inventions before the shipping container homes weren't big enough to take in too many goods and supplies.

Now, the shipping containers are big enough to house tons of weights, and at the same time, small enough to be transported via wheels. They are also very strong, and at the same time, light enough to be carried by pulleys. These container homes were made possible by important figures like McLean, who in 1980 helped solve the problem of transportation between countries that were in no way proximal to each other. McLean, who is also known as Henry Ford, started the business of transportation in 1934. In no time, he made enough money to buy five more trucks. So, one day, after watching people load and unload cargoes into ships with so much effort, he got the idea to create containers that could be arranged in ships in large numbers.

McLean and Keith Tantlinger were able to adjust the containers by having them refined and tested accordingly. They then came up with a container that was easy to load and unload, theft-resistance (it could be locked), and highly sturdy. McLean's creation began to create a sensation when companies began to place orders from different parts of the world, as it cut about twenty-five percent of the cost incurred on the loading and unloading of ships. They were also attracted by the fact that they could tone down the rate at which theft occurred by locking up the containers.

The first ship ever to load a container was the Gateway city, and it traveled from New Jersey to Miami. This time, only two workers were needed to load the container, which was a massive improvement. Later on, McLean dealt with the issue of standardization so that goods could be uniformly stacked within the containers with as much ease as possible. The following observations were also made with respect to the new shipping containers.

- The cost incurred on shipping cargo dropped by a percentage greater than ninety percent.
- Cargo that once cost five dollars per ton to load can now be loaded for a price that is not even equivalent to a dollar.
- Between 1966 and 1983, the number of countries that used the containers rose from a percentage of one to about ninety percent.
- There are about nineteen million shipping containers in the world today.

Drawbacks of a Shipping Container Home

To help you ascertain if a shipping container home is what you indeed want, a few of the challenges a shipping container home may pose to you are discussed below.

1. Dimensions of the inner compartments: Containers have one thing similar to them all; the breadth of the structure. They have different heights and lengths, but then, the width never really exceeds eight feet. Consequently, due to extra paddings and ornate coverings, you could end up having the width of the container slashed down by one foot. And really, if you don't take time to outline how you want to have things arranged, you might have issues with spacing. This issue even gets more pronounced if you have a large family. But then, to solve this issue, you could just stack two or three more containers next to each other and connect them with adjoining doors. But then, eventually, it all boils down to the money you can spare.

2. The position of insulator materials and structures: Planning out a source of insulation for your container home is one consequential factor you must consider if you plan on living in some areas with not too nice climatic factors. Certainly, you would desire some padding that prevents the sun's heat from occupying the interior. The insulation pad could be placed either outside or inside your container and because you can't leave the padding uncovered, you'd still need to have it covered. This issue usually leads to the consumption of useful space within your container, and that could become another issue with space.

3. Utility compartments: The issue with these housing structures is that you couldn't possibly have all the facilities (electrical wirings, plumbing connections, ceilings, floors) you need inside it. Surely, you could have some of them, but most times, it can't be all. As regards electricity, you could easily get wire strings of small diameter

that could easily be hidden in the walls of your container. The real issue comes when you have to consider your plumbing works. Conduits for waste and liquid drains are usually thick and with wide pipes, the little space you have may be encroached. In most cases, these pipes are usually passed through the floor or ceilings.

4. Confusing building codes: Some of the codes related to container homes include you being able to determine the location for them. Most times, the codes get so confusing that you could even need to make a few changes to the design you want to implement in your container. However, all of this hassle gets solved if you can lay your hands on some professional builder.

5. Finding professional contractors can be one very difficult task: Even for those who decorate their containers themselves, they usually would at one point or the other need to call on to some professional who would help them fix one or two things. Finding a very interested contractor in

what you want to do is one very vital requirement, and it could get pretty hard finding one that wouldn't cut corners while working. But then, it all gets good with the shipping companies out there that can help you monitor one or two things for the best possible outcome.

6. The outlook of the shipping container home: Many controversies have been raised regarding container homes, and most of them are staked on mere ignorance. This issue is often not regarded as a potential issue until you actually get a container home for yourself.

7. Health: Several havocs could be posed on those who live in these containers for the sole purpose of it being metallic. Others include electrocution via lightning and the inhalation of toxic paint chemicals. However, the issue with chemicals in paint can be solved if you limit the usage to friendly concentrations. You could also leave the container for a long while to allow the choking smell to leave. As for the issue with lightning strikes, you would be good to go once you have

your container adequately grounded. You could also seek the help of a professional electrician who would see to it that you are well-protected.

Why Choose a Shipping Container Home?

There are many reasons you would want to have a shipping container home for yourself, and below are a few of the reasons.

1. Shipping container homes are pocket-friendly: Most times, all the money that is gulped by a shipping container construction includes the cost of whatever design you choose to work with, the size of your container, and a couple of other factors. Here, we will look at a few factors that differentiate the shipping container from other housing elements.
    - The roof: A shipping container already has an external covering at the top that serves as the roof. So, you don't have to spend money purchasing wood or corrugated sheets.

- Walls: Traditional buildings usually need that you get concrete, sand, or granite to construct the walls. However, shipping containers already have walls made of metallic surfaces. These ones are usually durable and might not need many embellishments, except you want to go aesthetic.
- Foundation: Shipping containers are usually supported at the bottom with sturdy structures at the four edges. With that, you won't even have to spend so much money planning out or constructing an actual foundation.
- Flooring: Parquet is one kind of flooring that you could work out on your container's floor, and that comes out more cheaply than actual concrete, tiled, or marble floors.

2. Shipping containers can be sustained: The term sustainability has to do with a structure not posing any risk to the environment in the form of pollution or any other unfortunate issue. This is where the reuse, reduce, and recycle keywords come to play. Shipping containers are ways by

which metal scraps and different useful materials can be reused. Ordinarily, these scraps of metals could have contributed to the waste of valuable space, but with this new invention, it all changes. It will also effectively reduce the cost of building constructions, as you could instead build more eye-catchy structures with metals.

3. Shipping containers are strong: If anything is going to be exposed to the salty tides of the ocean, they'd need to be as strong and sturdy as Mount Everest itself. This is one very beautiful feature that shipping contains possess. They are resistant to wear and tear and can bear tons of weight. A shipping container will single-handedly bear about nine thousand pounds of weight. Most importantly, come out being able to stand the test of time—about thirty years (if new) or fifteen years (if it's fairly used). Most times, the only damage most shipping containers actually suffer is the scratch or dent along their surfaces. Another beautiful thing about these structures is

that you don't have to worry about pests like termites that eat wood.

4. Shipping containers have exclusively unique features: The uniqueness of a shipping container is not attached to the container itself. What in actual reality bears the uniqueness is the brilliant thing you can work out with the container. All of these containers usually have the same dimensions—length, breadth, and height—but then, you could furnish the interiors with ceiling beams, paint, plywood, concrete, tiles, or marble. You could also control how much heat your shipping container absorbs and radiates by painting it with bold colors that would reflect the heat away. You could also try interesting techniques like bridging, vertical arrangements, and so on! As we go down in this discussion, all of these things will be highlighted.

5. Shipping containers don't follow a rigid sequence: Your containers can be used in any way you want, and so, you don't have to go by the 'home' feature attached to it. It can be used in

industries and several other areas! You could also have them brought to you in whatever location you are in. They are containers that are usually shipped over long distances. You could also make a home out of it as soon as possible without following a long list of instructions. As time goes on, you could also widen your container by adding more to the initial structure. Then, with doors joining each of the structures together, you would be free to go.

Chapter 2

Tips To Know Before Starting The Process

The tips discussed here will help you ensure that your shipping container home adventure starts off on the right track so that you can be proud of the eventual outcome. Let's take a look at them.

1. Check out the container before you purchase it: Just like you wouldn't buy an actual house without first checking the interior and the exterior, you should also ensure that you do the same for containers. But then, most times, you might not be able to completely scrutinize a shipping container especially when it is located at the other end of the world. However, it's a good thing we now live in a technological age. Ensure that you request for pictures that would help your scrutiny. Usually, the ones you would get at less high prices have routed the sea several times. So, you could find a lot of rusts and dents across the surface. The more expensive ones are usually

in great shape and might be just what you want to get if you are aiming at longevity.
2. Get yourself acquainted with the restrictions as regard building codes: Several communities are against the construction of shipping containers as homes. So, before you purchase one, ensure that you peruse the codes guiding your local areas. Get an understanding of the different bodies that govern the building of containers, the things you are allowed to do with them, the options of design you can work with, and so on. States like California and Texas are pretty much receptive to containers.
3. Have an insulation plan ready: Without proper insulation, your shipping container will be very hot during the summer and very cold during the winter. So, ensure that you make inquiries about insulation techniques from contractors before you get your container. For example, insulation that is done in a blanket style may need an interior stud wall. There are several options you could go for anyway.
4. Get a contractor that can oversee the whole construction process: Seek the help of someone

who knows his onions regarding shipping container homes.

5. Protection for your shipping containers: If you are getting a container to live in, you might need to modify a few features while considering that they were originally structured for water bodies. So, the wood used for the flooring is usually coated heavily with pesticides that help to keep rodents away from the goods kept in them. The paint also contains toxic chemicals that protect the body of the container from the salty environment of the sea. To solve this problem, you could opt for new containers with little to no chemicals. Insulating the walls of your container with foam can also help to solve this problem.

6. Do not cut your container into pieces: This issue usually would arise when you have to cut out holes for doors when you want to adjoin two or more containers. Even though the structures are very rigid and strong, you cutting into them would gradually reduce their general strength. This issue could lead to you having to spend more than you planned to support the cut parts.

7. Make strategies for plumbing and electrical works: You will need to plan out ports and channels for conduits, pipes, and wires. So, before you start with interior decorations, get your contractor to cut out appropriate holes for this purpose.
8. You should know how to tell containers apart: Contrary to many opinions, shipping containers are not exactly the same. The regular shipping containers are usually about eight feet in height and the cubical ones with additional feet. This factor could lead to space issues if ignored, as things like insulation eat a lot into whatever space you originally have to yourself.
9. Get ready for the effects of the wind: If you are having your container positioned at a point where there is a lot of wind, you might need to make a few modifications to avoid unnecessary noises in your home. To avoid this issue, ensure that you place your container in an area protected from the breeze's violent waves. That is why securing a location for your container even before you procure the container is very important.

10. Ensure you do not employ too many welding techniques in your container: Welding is one technique that plays out when you work with more than one container. If you have to join them, ensure that you reduce the amount of welding you have to work with. Like it was pointed out earlier, excessive welding will reduce the sturdiness of your container.
11. Consider all of your options before getting your container: One thing about these containers is their weight, so if you are transporting them to where you need your container to be, you might end up exerting a lot of pressure on the soil. This issue could lead to the destruction of the structure of the soil. Shipping containers are usually very great if the final location is close to a port.
12. Get ready for an extra cost and miscellaneous expenses: Most people would opt for a container home because of the reduced cost attached. But then, in actual reality, things like welding, insulations, embellishments, flooring, and others could pull out of your pocket the same amount of money that the construction of a regular house would pull out.

Chapter 3

Planning Your Home Layout

One beautiful part of getting a container is the fact that it allows you the grace of implementing your own ideas and bringing your imaginations to life! With the right planning, you could easily convert a metallic structure into something much more fascinating by fusing the right compartments, equipment, and furnishes. In this chapter, we will discuss a few home plans to help you maximize your container home to a great extent.

Plan 1: Empty Nester

- The Empty Nester plan is one architectural design that comprises a bedroom at the ground level and an extra row above for the kitchen and bathroom.
- This plan is executed in a 40-inch container.

- The kitchen outlined here can fully house the regular kitchen appliances, and usually, it comes with different kinds of finish techniques.
- The bathroom also features a walk-in shower.

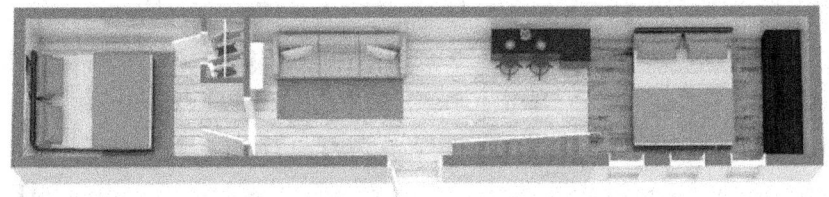

Plan 2: Happy Twogether

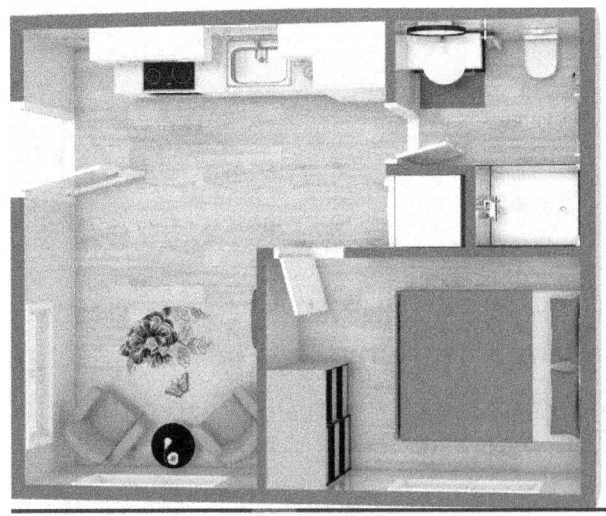

- The Happy Twogether is a design that can be implemented with two containers.
- The containers should be about twenty inches with about three hundred square feet of space internally.
- There's a full bedroom on the ground floor.
- There's a living room that adjoins a wide kitchen.
- The bathroom features a walk-in shower.
- There's a thirty-six-inch vanity toilet.

Plan 3: Dwell Well

- The Dwell Well plan can be implemented with two containers.
- It uses containers of forty inches and twenty inches and a total of 480-square feet.

- This plan offers a kitchen of a pretty large size. This feature is good for those who plan on using their containers for this major purpose.
- There's a bedroom on the ground floor.
- There's a sophisticated bedroom that is equipped with a washer and a dryer.

Plan 4: Double Duo

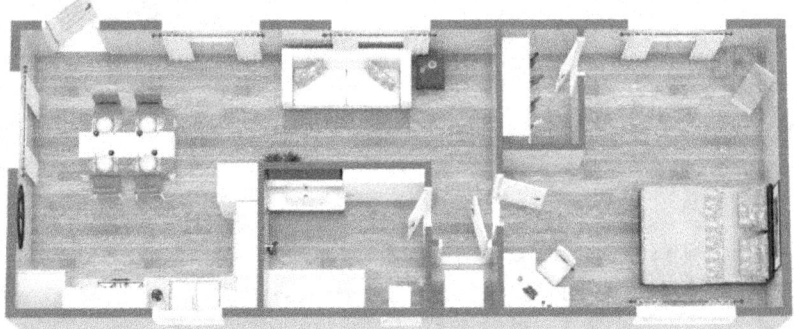

- The Double Duo plan can be implemented with two containers.
- It utilizes two containers of forty inches each and a total of 640-square feet.
- It has one large-sized bedroom, and it is equipped with a walk-in closet.
- It has a generously sized kitchen.
- It has a generously sized living room.
- The bathroom has a bathtub in it

- There's enough space for the washer and dryer in the bathroom.
- This plan allows for a double bedroom plan, i.e., two rooms.

Plan 5: Family Matters 2 Bedroom

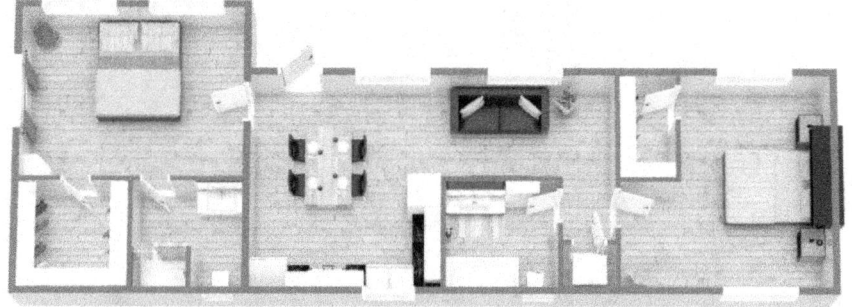

- The Family Matters 2 Bedroom utilizes two containers
- Each of the containers has a dimension of forty inches and a total of 640-square feet.
- This plan features two bedrooms, each with a closet attached.
- There's a generously sized kitchen.
- There's a bathroom that is equipped with a bathtub.
- In the bathroom is enough space for a washer and a dryer.

- This version is also available in a one-bedroom style.

Plan 6: Roommates
- This is a plan that is utilized with just a container.
- The container has a length of 20-inches.
- There are two sleeping compartments big enough for a full-sized bed.
- There's a kitchenette—a small kitchen.
- There's a bathroom.

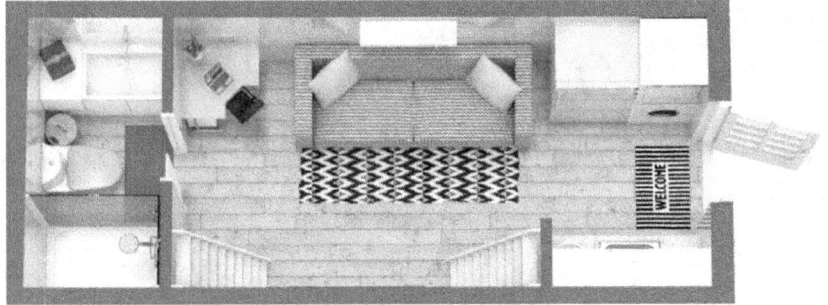

Chapter 4

Choosing The Right Container

One of the most important steps for you to build your container is getting the right one. The container you get is what determines the result of whatever embellishments you make. Most people make the mistake of thinking that all containers are of the same structural integrity, so they just buy anyone. However, if you plan to avoid issues with your container after buying it, you might need to pay attention to the following details.

Why is Container Condition Important?

Just before paying for a container, you need to know its condition. You might wonder why this is so important, though. First, checking it out will help you ensure that it is in the right shape. You will also ascertain if it is of a size that caters to all the structural designs you plan on implementing. Here, you will be able to determine the type—either a general-purpose container or a dry van container—and the size you want—either a 20-foot or 40-foot container.

Next, you might want to know what condition you need your container to be in. Like it was discussed earlier, the cheap ones are usually not as much in good condition as the expensive ones. However, you need to note that buying the ones of less quality will do nothing to help you save your money. At the end of the day, you end up spending more money repairing the containers when they become weak or rusty. You can check out the condition of a container by inspection, and for safety, you might want to do the checking yourself.

When Should a Container be Inspected?

Just before you start your project on a container, you have to set out a time to inspect it. Skipping this step usually would lead to you spending much more than you planned consequently.

Guidelines For Pre-purchase Inspection

Checking out your container before you buy it will be very helpful because it helps you know the state of what you are getting beforehand. Inspection gets very easy when you lived somewhere close to the location of the containers. This way, you could find your way there and perform the inspection personally. However, if you aren't in close proximity, you could opt for an inspection via video or photo. Most times, videos and pictures may not provide clear and descriptive information on what you need, so you'd mostly be taking a whole lot of risks.

Guidelines For Post-Purchase Inspection

This inspection is one that you carry out when you get your container delivered to your site. For this process to work out, you have to ensure that you are present when the container is delivered. If you cannot be there, you should get someone knowledgeable about containers to be there in your place. Ensure they are trustworthy. At this point, you could have paid fully or in parts. You will need to sign a form that attests to the fact that you are now in the custody of the container. Before you sign, though, you have to ensure that you have carried out all the necessary inspections. If you notice something wrong, ensure that you commune with the driver at once, or better still, get in contact with the supplier. This step would be best done before the container is offloaded. So, the beauty of this stage is in you being able to catch a err soon enough.

How and What to Inspect?

While inspecting, you have to ensure that you peruse each area with your head and your eyes incline towards the direction of inspection. For example, while inspecting the floor, ensure you check from left to right and from the front to the back. You might also need to take a couple of tools like a selfie stick with a shutter button that is within the reach of your fingers. This will enable you to properly scan the parts your hands can't reach out to. For the interior, you could go with a flashlight or torch. Ladders will help you access the beams and the roofs of your structures. Then, lastly, you could use a hammer to check how severely rust has eaten into the container.

Structural Frame

Bear in mind that the power of any container is borne by the twelve steel beams that make the edges of the container's faces. These beams are of various sizes and cross-cuts—corner beams, bottom rails, and top rails. Note that any damage to the beam cannot be fixed easily, so you need to view how they are faring thoroughly. If you notice superficial rusts, you need not worry much. Deep rusts are of much more concern.

Underside

The underside is one part of a container that you probably won't notice. It is composed of beams that transversely run across the breadth of the container and its bottom rails. This structure is what the wooden floor of the container is attached to. The containers with 40-foot have a tunnel with a gooseneck at one end. That end is the one that is designed to screw into the trailers that transport the container. The underside is usually the closest to the ground, so there is a high possibility you find them heavily rusted.

Inspecting the underside also presents difficulty in that it cannot be easily accessed. However, you could make use of the method the driver uses to offload the container. While it is halfway down, you could hastily take a couple of pictures. However, ensure that you do not stand directly under the halfway suspended container. This will be a great time to make maximum use of your selfie-stick, though. If you notice damage, you could easily fix it.

Walls

This part of a container is the part that you can easily access. They are usually constructed out of steel and are in corrugated forms. It is the steel that brackets the interiors. Rusts and dents on the walls can be neglected as long as it isn't too intense. To pick out areas suffering primarily from rust, you could hit it with a hammer or other metallic tool. Having flakes fall off is a huge sign of deep rusts, which can be a serious issue. The holes can often be patched, but then, rusts that bring flakes could be a good sign that more holes will arise. Another thing that could save you when the container is heavily rusted is if the plans for your windows and doors coincide with the areas with the rust.

Roof

The roof of a container is constructed out of folded metals, and its design is a bit different from the ones used for the construction of the walls. The best way to check the roof of a container is by climbing with a ladder. In case there's no ladder, you could opt for pictures taken with selfie-sticks. The first thing you should be on the lookout for are signs of patches or dents. Hitting the surface with a hammer can be one effective method of determining whether the rust patterns are deep or superficial. While doing this, ensure that your body weight isn't directed totally to the flaky parts. Checking to see if your container's roof is waterproof is done during the inspection of the interior.

End Doors

The end doors and other parts tied to the component should be the only mobile part of your container.

Anything else that doesn't fall into the bracket and yet, has mobile properties must have gotten affected by factors like dirt and rust at one point or the other. To know if the end doors are in good condition, move the four lock knobs and then watch how they rotate around their axis. You also need to be sure that the cams and keepers are in a tight joint. Next, check out the doors to know how much allowances the hinges allows.

Interior

The interior check is more or less a situation where you access the other side of the exteriors you accessed previously. So, while checking, ensure that you check the same things you checked while checking the exterior. To get a good look at these interior parts, you might want to go with a flashlight that would easily eradicate the dark points. To know if there are holes in the container that can cause water to leak in, close the door of the container, and then check if there's a reflection of light from any angle. If you notice any streaks of light, you can easily get that corrected by blocking it thinly with cement or any other adhesive.

Floor

Most of the containers out there have floors made from plywood, and it has high absorbing power. In cases where chemicals at one time spilled on the floor, it would totally absorb the constituents. So, to be on the safe side, you can detect this by taking note of how the inner space of the container smells when the door is shut. Most of these chemicals have a sharp and pungent smell that you'd notice almost immediately. While doing this, ensure that you do not sniff too deeply, as it can pose a lot of risk to your lungs. You should only go on to deep sniffing when the shallow one does not fetch you a suspicious response. Also, to be on the safe side, you could try going with someone else who could help you to easily detect strange and unnatural scents. Note that the harm posed by a chemical exists in its concentrations. So, if you are in a position where you can choose between containers, choose the one with the faintest smell. Also, if you manage to catch the smell of mold, it can only imply a leak in the container. Most times, the leak issues come out as being already solved, but then, ensure you find out the area it is in. If you do not plan to make any changes to your container's floor, ensure that there aren't any large holes or broken wooden fragments.

Documentation

You can get to know where your container has been to and the records of ownership transfers that have been made to it by getting yourself acquainted with some important documents. Here, we will study a few of them and see what information they actually have to offer.

CSC Plate

The CSC plate is also known as the Combined Data Plate. It is the part of the container containing so many helpful details, and you will find it fixed to the metallic plate with statutory information. The CSC plate contains several information, and a few of them include the;

1. Container Identification Number: This number includes details like;
   - Owner Prefix
   - Equipment familiarizer.
   - Serial code
   - Check digit, etc. This digit is used to ensure that the CIN is set down accurately. Inputting the wrong BIC code when calculating can fetch you the wrong digit.
2. Type Code: This code has four digits, but then, a few of the extra numbers or letters you'd see there are tied to particular manufacturers. For

example, a code like 22G1 means your container has a normal height and a breadth of about twenty feet. It's also a general-purpose container.
3. Classification Society Approval: This document makes useful references to the groups that take charge of the approval of your container. Here, an example of a reference is AB-447/02-06. It stands for the American Bureau of Shipping which was approved in February 2006, with a number of 447.
4. ACEP/PES: The plate usually will have a spot for the ACEP number or the dates of the first and last checks run on the container by the PES society.

Conditions and Container Grades

Getting someone who is into the sales or purchases of containers can help you know the accurate condition of your container. Usually, they have ideas on what to look out for, the quality of things to expect and so much more. To get off on the right foot, you could start by getting yourself acquainted with the guidelines that affect the grade of your container. Most times, the grades also speak more of the outer appearance rather than the strength inherent in your container. The strength factor is usually less important to those that want to build homes. To understand the grading of containers more, we will classify them under a few brackets.

New (and New-ish) Containers

These containers are known as the 'one-trip' containers. They are usually at their newest forms, and usually, could come at very exorbitant prices, at least, more than the used or old ones. The new containers usually are directly from the producer and have never really been used to move goods across the ocean or any other thing. However, you may find out that it has a CSC plate attached to it, and that is because it still has to be shipped to reach wherever you are. The other kinds of new containers with a lower grade look new and refurbished. They are not exactly new, so, of course, you get the drift. All new containers usually have neat interiors, but you may sometimes find the slightest scratches across the outer surface. Those scratches usually occur due to the way they are handled and moved at ports.

One-Trip Containers

These containers, in some cases, could be an interchangeable term for new, but then, the containers aren't exactly new. Why? Before you get the container, it usually would have been used to transport goods across the ocean once. Then, the moment they arrive at their destined coordinates, whoever owns them could decide to sell them off. This method is because most people don't find the sense in transporting a bunch of empty containers across the ocean when several commodities and goods could be stacked in there. That is why these containers usually would be sold with a discount for the buyers.

Refurbished Containers

This kind of container is more like a renovated house. The containers usually would have previously suffered one or two things, so the broken parts are usually brought together, then patched, or better still, replaced. Sometimes, it's just the walls that are recoated with paint, and other times, a few parts of the container are replaced with a new one. Dirt, spills, and rusts are examples of some other things that can be taken off the surface of the container. Then, in a situation where the doors and bolts have certain issues, they could be changed to make things nice and shiny.

Used Containers

A used container is one that brackets all containers that have both been used to the core or those that have sparingly been used. Usually, these containers have been used for about ten to thirteen years, and by that time, they would have been subjected to a lot of damage, wear and tear, and some other factors that might need intense replacement. These containers are usually tagged as wind-tight or, preferably, watertight.

Cargo Worthy (CW) Containers

These are containers that are certified by the CSC. Usually, they could suffer one or two facial defects, but they do the same things that a new container would do for you. Most times, defects in a container like a broken window or a door usually reduce the qualifications of the container and then make it cargo-unworthy. So, you'd find that cargo-worthy containers are the ones usually in a condition good enough to be moved across the ocean.

As-Is Containers

These containers are usually not up to the standards of a cargo-worthy container, as they have one or two obvious damage. They are containers that are so old that the seller usually avoids spending the time and money to have them inspected. Before you buy this kind of container, please get clear pictures or probably access the container personally. That way, you'd be sure of what you are getting because most of them are pretty much in bad shape. Most of the container dealers usually do not sell these kinds of containers, and the ones who do would hardly offer a warranty term.

Reasons to Choose New and (New-ish) Containers

Just in case you decide to go for these types of containers, a few reasons to help you make your choice are discussed here.

1. New containers are uniform: Uniformity is one thing you need to look out for if you are using your container for residential purposes. Everything is usually straight up and in good shape, and you won't really have to deal with rust or paint issues. The beauty of uniformity comes when you order for more than a container.
2. Outlook: With how beautiful they usually would look, no one would really be bothered about their presence in the area. What usually would get people talking is them seeing an old and rusty container!
3. Lifespan: You would discover that new and new-ish containers can be used for a pretty long period before they begin to deteriorate. They usually can stand the test of time. This reason is one of the big

reasons most people would go for a new container.

4. The Peace of Mind: Getting a new container is beneficial because you would not have to worry about dealing with broken parts or components or some other issue. You'd find out that since they have never really been used before, the floors would contain no form of chemicals that would be dangerous to your health. And if the container was once used to move chemicals of very high toxicity, the company would have it specifically marked so that you'd know.

Reasons to Choose Used Containers

And if used containers are what you have in mind, then a couple of reasons to help you make this decision are given here.

1. They are cheap: At least, in comparison with the new containers, the used ones come out as cheaper. And this factor doesn't really matter much since the containers are just of a little lower grade than the new ones.
2. They can easily be gotten: Used containers can be found anywhere and everywhere! However,

what usually streamlines the wide range of choices you have is their inherent quality. Some of these used ones are of higher quality than the others, and so you might need to exercise a little bit of care when picking them out. Another angle from which we could view the benefit of their accessibility is that it helps you get your project done much quicker. New containers, when ordered, would have to first be constructed, and that involves time. The One-trip containers too could be hard to find, and the refurbished ones will also need to be renovated.

3. Used containers are friendly to the environment: This factor stands as one of the biggest benefits that a used container would bring to you. For a used container, you would not be working with raw materials or any other factor that would require you to extract raw materials from the earth. All you are mostly going to be doing is to use and recycle. This factor could even fetch you a tax incentive along the way.

Cost of Shipping Containers

This section is one of the many questions most people usually ask. And usually, the price of a shipping container depends on factors like;

1. The location
2. The age
3. The type
4. The condition

To help you decide on the choices to make, we will be listing a few of the available options here. Some of the price ranges could be a little bit more or less than what you see here, though.

1. The used and standard twenty-feet container: $2000
2. The Newish and Standard twenty-feet container: $3100
3. The used and Standard forty-feet container: $2850
4. The Newish and Standard forty-feet container: $5,600
5. The used and high-cubed twenty-feet container: $2100
6. The newish and high-cubed twenty-feet container: $3100

7. The used and high-cubed forty-feet container: $2900
8. The newish and high-cubed forty-feet container: $5700

The Condition of Shipping Container to Buy

Here, your attention will be slowly drawn to the condition of the shipping container you are to look out for. It is also the stage where you need to consider their respective advantages, disadvantages, and the amount of money they can be bought for. To ease things, we have set a few questions you would want to ask yourself as you make your plans.

1. Do you plan on moving your container after it has been shipped over to you? Do you plan on leaving the container in a place forever? If your response is positive, then you should look for CW containers.
2. How does your project look like? What is the outline like? Is it one that requires a lot of windows and doors? If your answer is positive, you have to ensure that you go for a container that is highly strong. Like it was stated earlier, the cutting of windows and extra doors out of your

container will only tamper with its structural integrity.
3. Do you plan to erect another roof above the container? If your answer here is positive, you will most likely not need to worry about the damage to the roof you noticed during inspection. Water leakage issues or holes in the roof can be ignored too.
4. Are you bothered about general outward appearances? If your response here is positive, then you should go for the new or newish containers. The only time you should settle for any one in a lesser condition should be in a case where you plan on having your container refurbished by yourself.
5. Do you plan on replacing the floor of the container? Or do you plan on having another floor erected over the original floor? If your response here is positive, you really do not need to bother about the damage done to the floors by chemicals or spills.

Where to Buy Your Containers

Once you have made conclusions regarding all that has been discussed above, you might need to figure out where you plan on buying the container. First-time buyers usually would have many issues in this area as each of the sellers out there has their respective advantages and disadvantages. There are many dealers out there in the market, and sometimes, you could get overwhelmed and not even know where to start from. So, here, a little help will be offered, assuming that you have already decided on the type of container you are getting and the size.

Now, being able to point out what you want and knowing where you can find it are two different things. There usually are several options you can work with, and it all depends on where you are and some other choices that are up to you. Now that you know the size and the cost of what you need, you can move on to fishing it right out. You would notice that several of these dealers are ones that you would find on the internet. In fact, it doesn't really matter whether you get your container via the internet or not. What really matters is that the internet will still play a big role in helping you find what is right for you.

Online—In The US

Several online dealers in the United States are just excellent dealers as regards containers. However, we will be recommending one very good dealer to you—Box hub. A few points to note about getting your containers online in the US.

1. You can find your container inventory anywhere in the world.
2. You get to price your containers live.
3. You can finish off the transaction online without having to leave your house!
4. You can get your money back if you aren't pleased with what it eventually delivered to you.
5. They work closely with the prominent shipping lines, so you may not have to suffer the effects of having middlemen involved. The lesser the parties in the line of production, the lesser the price is, and the easier for you.
6. You can easily find all the prices of their containers on the internet.
7. You don't need to fill any form or make long calls to price your containers.

8. They can help you to deliver whatever choice you finally make to your location at a cost.
9. With Box Hub, you end up saving more money than you planned.

To get a useful list of other dealers, you could try searching for 'Shipping Containers in Miami.' Google usually would fetch you pretty good responses. And if you don't want Miami, you could just type in any other city, preferably the one you live in. If you are purchasing from someone that does not deal with containers, it is recommended that you go physically to check out the quality of the container. The only issue here is that you are most likely responsible for the pickup and delivery.

Online — Outside The US

For those that live outside the United States, you can still get the container you desire. Almost every country has access to shipping containers via their seaports and other places. To find a seaport near you, you could try using the 'Sea Rate Website.' It helps you scour hundreds of ports within your location and provide means by which you can contact them and other information like the size and the port's capacity. Apart from seaports, you could also work with the land ports.

To find the ones around you, you could just search on the internet using credible websites like Craiglist.

China is one country that offers new and one-trip containers. To get directly in touch with Chinese dealers, you could try buying directly from sites like Alibaba. Usually, the purchase doesn't come out as good as buying from where you are, as you may need to monitor the movement of the container, settle all the necessary paperwork, and several other things. To ease things, you could also resort to working with dealers of containers in the place you reside in.

Finding Containers Offline

There are several containers that exist all over the place with no use for them at all. It's either because they are filled with some worthless materials or that they have been long forgotten. So, if you find one you really like, you could meet up with the owner and discuss your plans to purchase it. They would most likely be pleased to discuss that topic with you, though, as they finally get to get rid of it and, in the process, make some cool money. So, while making those walks, hikes, or drives, stay as alert as possible.

You could also get useful referrals from people you know that work in areas connected to shipping and transport. Most times, they could know one or two people in the business that can help you get what you want. If the people you know don't know anyone, ask if someone they know knows about the business. Somehow, along the line, you might be lucky enough to find one.

What To Lookout For When Choosing a Container Dealer

When choosing a container dealer, there are several things that you might want to consider, as each of these dealers has its respective good and bad sides. You surely do not want to be caught up in some messy situation, so, here, a few of these factors would be considered to help you out.

Integrity and Reputation

Container dealers, no doubt, have a better idea of their products than the buyer, so you might have to do your personal explorations and research to deal with this. Sometimes, it could get very difficult to get rid of the gap, but then, you should at least try because of issues like the sale of containers of very low quality and several others. So, it is very important that you find someone you can wholly trust in all of this. Trust is one factor that cannot be easily gained, so you might want to consider becoming a member of some reputable container organization like;

1. The Container Dealer's Association.
2. The Intermodal Association of North America.
3. The National Portable Storage Association.

Along the way, you might also be able to know what the others who have at one time purchased containers think as regards trusting the dealers. Sites like the Better Business Bureau and Yelp will go a long way to help with that. Reviews on Google sites will also help you fish out those dealers you can trust your containers with. You should also pay attention to the fact that bad reviews sometimes may be because of the difficulty of some customers. So, one of the best ways still is you communing with someone who once made a purchase.

One more thing you need to pay attention to is how you verify your purchase. Once you decide on the price that you want to get the container you desire, ensure that you get a copy of the BIC code and the CSC plate information of the container. The details will help you ascertain that the numbers recorded match the container you accessed.

Warranties and Returns

This factor is another of the very important ones. It is very necessary that you get hold of a dealer with the best warranty and return conditions. But then, while considering this factor, ensure that you pay attention to the part that calls for you to trust your dealer. For example, a few dealers would promise to offer you a lifetime warranty; this is one very unreal statement. Some other dealers may offer you a wonderful warranty at an increased price, and honestly, it is not a very feasible option.

Understanding the charges and steps involved in a warranty is very important when you want to make a warranty claim on a damaged container. Questions like these should be paid attention to;

1. Which party pays for the shipment of the container back to the dealer?
2. How will the shipment of the container be handled?
3. Is there going to be a charge you'd need to settle to have your container back?
4. How much extra fees would you need to pay for the whole process?

Volume Discounts

You might want to consider this discount if you plan on getting more than one container. It is recommended that you buy all the containers from one dealer to avoid issues like non-uniformity and so on. This way, you could get a very nice discount on your bulk sales. Sometimes, the volume discount is something that your seller or dealer would disclose to you themselves. The other times, however, might require that you make negotiations on your part. Just bear in mind that the volume discount will have a lot of effects on the final price.

To have proper knowledge of this term, though, you might need to understand a couple of marketing terms.

1. Average customer value: This is the revenue that one customer will fetch a company; i.e., the revenue made per customer.
2. The Customer Acquisition Cost: This term refers to the average amount of costs incurred during marketing that a company gets for paying the customer.

You might not need to know the exact values of these factors, but then, it is very necessary that you understand that they differ from one company to the other. In summary, buying more containers than the number the regular customer will buy will save the company the 'Customer Acquisition Cost' that it would have spent on other customers. It is only normal that the company shares with you a fraction of that benefit in the form of volume discounts.

Value-Added Services

In the line of production, some people come as regular retailers, and others as value-added retailers. When it comes to the shipping of containers, the sellers can help you to do a whole lot of things like;

1. Delivery and Offloading
2. Custom painting
3. Fixing of the lockboxes
4. Fixing of the window and door frames
5. Insulation
6. Plumbing works
7. Electrical connections, etc.

Delivery and Offloading

This is a point where you need to decide who helps you deliver and offload your container. Most of the big container dealers out there have all the equipment needed for the process, and a few of them include tilt-bed trailers, pulleys, cranes, and so on. All of these things will generally help you to save more time and money. Another important thing to consider here is time. Go for sellers that operate on a large scale than those that do on a small scale if you are going to get many containers. For example, ordering nine containers from someone who only has two available will mean that you have to wait. So, there usually is a need for you to be careful while making the necessary choices.

Chapter 5

Site Preparation and Foundation

Site Preparation

Before your container is delivered to you, you need to make several preparations. Failure to plan this stage well enough could often result in spending a lot more than you originally planned. Most of the steps you take here aim to ensure that the site is well prepared to receive the container. So, to help you, we will discuss some things you need to cater for.

Deciding on Location

First, you need to decide where you want your container to be positioned. Which side in your land graph do you need it in? What factors should determine your decision? Let's answer these questions and more below.

Sun and Shade

The sun is one major factor that you must consider. On that cold morning, having the rays of the sun bath your skin can be a very nice feeling, but then, at times when everything and everywhere is hot, the sun isn't what anyone wants. So, while observing your geographical area, ensure that you choose spots that feed in light softly to the insides of your container. You might also want to get an air conditioning system if you plan on setting your container in a sunny region.

Placing your container under a shady area or under a couple of trees will surely go a long way to help, but then, most times, these trees shed off their leaves during the fall and winter. To make calculations regarding the height of the sun at any place you are in, you could use tools like Sun Calc. It works at any date and time and helps you to consider implementing things like roof shades or lids for your windows in your project.

Topography and Drainage

This factor has to do with the shape and slope of your land. Slope is a factor that helps you to understand how water will run off it when there's rain. You surely would not want to find water puddles or sticky mud surrounding your container, as that could be quite messy. This factor will also help you see how you can change the direction of the water flowing across the land. Water, unfortunately, can be a home for mosquitoes, and snakes, so you have to exercise a lot of caution here.

Views

This section is where you think of what you can see through the windows and the doors of your container. Sometimes, the view of a hill, valley or moving water body will only add to the beauty of your container. So, while placing your container, ensure that you incline it in a way that allows you to have a good view of your surroundings.

Access

Think of how you will want to get into the container from the major roads. How long do you want the pathway to be? At what angle of elevation should it be in? Should you include steeps or slopes? Do you need to get rid of any natural impediment from the way? Would you need to get rid of trees or other plants? Does the view get good or bad as you go up the road? You also would need to create a pathway that the building contractors and trailers can work with. It has to be wide enough and equipped with turns and angles that will make them have the best work output.

Site Work

This involves all the processes you will need to employ to ensure that your building site is ready for your container's placement. Here, you might need to follow a particular order so that you don't ruin one thing or the other. Let's discuss some activities that take place here.

Marking and Staking

This usually comes as the first thing that you need to do.

1. Mark the ends that your container will be erected in.
2. Mark the spots where the other things like utilities, roads, and buildings will be constructed on.
3. For marking, you could just make use of paint or wooden sticks connected with ropes.

Clearing and Grubbing

1. Clear the vegetation and debris off the land if there's any.
2. Get rid of trees, tree stumps, rocks, if there are any.
3. The more vegetation that covers the land, the more clearing you may need to do.

Grading, Cut, and Fill
1. Here, you can begin by choosing first a foundation for your container. You could either grade the floor uniformly or go with the uneven floor.
2. You could grade the land with concrete or raised slabs.
3. Add swales and berms to shield your container home from the effects of a flood.
4. Fix culverts, bridges, and low-water intersections at points where there is water flow.

Road Building
1. Top the roads leading to your container with fillers like gravel, asphalt, or concrete.
2. Avoid heavy equipment to prevent the roads from getting damaged.

Erosion Control
1. A land that has been cleared of vegetation and dirt is usually prone to erosion.
2. Erosion sometimes is caused by rain or the pile-up of sediments in ponds and streams.

3. You can control erosion by planting useful vegetation near the area your container is to sit on.
4. You could work with erosion control equipment like wattles and silt fences.
5. Check the Environmental Quality Office of your state to get the necessary information as regards erosion and water pollution.

Fencing and Security
1. Secure your container with container locks and grids.
2. You could build a fence around the container.
3. To build a fence, ensure that you mark out a line for it while you get things ready; building it before the container arrives would only limit the space for the dealers to work with.

Foundation

The kind of foundation you need for your container is an important factor to consider when constructing your container.

Is Foundation Required for Containers?

Foundation is necessary for your container as the ground usually undergoes shifts and slides, thereby affecting the level of your container home. A foundation will fetch you a stable and rigid leveling. It's even more important if you are working with many containers. A shift in the ground level can cause a separation of your containers. The area where you plan to put your container could also include some materials like rocks and clay that would only cause an unevenness of the floor level. However, a more leveled foundation will help the weight of your container to be evenly spread across the ground. Your container's bottom would also be safe from rust and moisture issues.

Types of Foundations For Containers

There are four major types of foundations that you can erect for your container, and they include pier, pile, stab, and strip. They are the regular and common ones, and so you might want to consider which is best for you.

Pier Foundation

1. They are the most common kinds of foundations for container homes.

2. It is cheap to construct and can be done single-handedly.
3. You can get it done in a little time.
4. This foundation is done with concrete blocks, with each of a diameter of 50cm by 50cm by 50cm.
5. The strength of the concrete is increased by supporting it with steel.
6. They're usually laid at the corners of the container.
7. You need four of them for twenty-feet containers, and for the forty-feet containers, you will need an extra two to support the middle.
8. Since you won't be digging up the earth, you get to save a lot of time and money.
9. The only digging you do is the one for the piers.
10. You do not need any special or technical tool or know-how to construct this kind of foundation.

Pile Foundation

1. This foundation works best for weak soils.
2. Here, you push in piles through the weak soil until you get to the point that is a bit more rigid and stable.

3. Once you get the piles on solid ground, go on to keep them in place with a lot of concrete.
4. This is not something you can do yourself. You may need help and technical know-how.
5. An example of a tool needed for this foundation is the pile driver.

Slab Foundation

1. This is a foundation that is also done on soils with low-carrying capacity.
2. It takes time to erect one.
3. You will need to dig up a lot of soil.
4. Here, you make a concrete slab for your containers.
5. For a 40-feet container, work with an 18-feet wide by a 42-feet long slab. This dimension will help to offer an extra layer of foundation outside the area occupied by your container.
6. It provides rigidity and stability to your container.
7. You don't have to worry about issues related to termite attacks.
8. They are more expensive to erect.

9. They are constructed in areas where the climate is warm, as the slabs help transfer the heat in the container to the ground below.
10. However, you may not easily access any connections you make below the ground with a slab foundation, e.g., wires or pipes. Most times, you may have to break up the slab.

Strip Foundation

1. This is also known as the trench foundation.
2. It is a fuse of the ideas employed in the pier and slab foundations.
3. Here, a strip of concrete is constructed to support the container.
4. The concrete strip is usually about two feet wide and four feet deep.
5. You can choose to make the strips for the outer edges of the container or at the top and bottom lines.
6. It is cheaper with respect to the slab foundation, though, not as firm.
7. You could run a rubble strip below the strip foundation in a case where the ground is usually wet and loose.

8. This foundation is resistant to earthquakes.
9. They are the best foundation for small and medium-sized containers.

Strength of Foundation Concrete to Use

This section is highly important for you if you chose to work with the pier or slab foundation. Your technical engineer usually determines the strength of the concrete to use. Usually, what is preferred is one of a C-value. For example, a C15 concrete can be made with one part of cement, two parts of sand, and five parts of gravel. The more cement you utilize when working, the stronger the foundation comes out to be. A C-30 concrete is a very strong concrete.

If you want to mix just a little bit of concrete, you could work with your hand or some other simple mixing tool. However, it is recommended that you have the concrete mixed for you by some site workers and then delivered to you for larger portions. To know how much concrete you will be working with, simply calculate the cubic meters of your foundation. For example, construct a slab foundation about ten feet wide, twenty-two feet long, and two feet deep, multiply the figures and order whatever you get. In this case, you have to order four hundred and forty cubic feet of concrete.

Attaching Containers to Foundations

You can attach a container to the foundation you have made for it by working with a steel plate in a casting operation. The casting operation usually involves you fixing the steel plate to the supports of the container with the use of concrete. You could also use epoxy instead of cement. You could also just choose to place the container unto the foundations directly, but then, there always comes the issue of floods and violent winds.

Chapter 6

Insulating The Container

Insulating your container is one vital step to take to make your container home a suitable place for you to live.

What is Insulation?

Insulation can be defined as a material that helps prevent the movement of heat via the walls of your container. This way, the heat from outside can't find its way in, and the one inside won't be able to find its way out. For example, when you turn on the conditioning system, you ensure that all the windows and doors are closed to allow cooling on the interiors of a room. Usually, opening the door leads to some chilled air in the room being replaced by the heat from outside. In this kind of situation, the walls will serve as insulation that prevents the movement of heat. Insulating materials will help to cage molecules of air and some other gases within tiny cells and paths. The best insulator you might want to use should be in a gaseous form due to its inability to conduct heat energy.

Why Insulate Your Container?

The moment you get your container insulated, it means you have succeeded in creating a distinction between the air inside the container and the air outside. So, in simpler terms, the heat that exists in the warm regions cannot find its way to the cool regions. This principle will largely help you raise your container's efficiency by reducing the energy needed to regulate the internal temperature. You also want to bear in mind that the containers are constructed from steel, and that is one metal that comes as a great conductor of heat. So, during summer, if your container is not well insulated, the heat from the sun can be channeled into your container, leading to an increase in the temperature.

Climatic Effects of Your Insulation Choice

Climate is the weather condition at a particular period of time, and it is also a very important factor that should push you to insulate your container. Sometimes, when the weather is very cold, you might need to heat up your container. You wouldn't want a situation where the heat being generated gets transferred to the external environment. You'd want it trapped within the walls of the container to feel the proper warmth, yes? Yes. But then, if you live in a place with the best climatic conditions, i.e., one that is neither too hot nor too cold, you don't really need to insulate your container.

Placing Your Container Insulation

Now that you have decided to insulate your container, you must decide where you want it to be. You would notice that several buildings usually have pads that separate the outer walls from the inner walls. Usually, these pads are materials that provide your container with properties like its shape, its resistance to fire, shield from adverse weather conditions, thermal insulation, and so on. All you now need to do is decide where you want this insulation to be positioned in the container.

One of the best places to place your insulation is within the inner walls, right inside the container. The stud walls usually come out as extra space to run your pipes and electrical wire strings. They can also be used when you need to do some other interior attachments. But then, some people actually see the exteriorly placed insulation as a better option. If that is what you prefer, ensure that you have it covered with a protective covering that would help you to protect the insulation from harsh weather conditions.

What to Consider When Choosing Your Insulation

There are several kinds of insulation that you could choose to work with when insulating your container. Here, we will discuss important tips to guide you in your choice of insulation.

- The general performance of the insulation
    1. An insulation's general performance is determined by factors like the material, the gas trapped between the walls, etc.

2. The R-value is a measure of how the material can avoid the transmission of heat energy through a given length.
3. Air leakage. This is a measure of how the insulation can stop air molecules from passing through it.
4. Vapor permeability. This is a measure of how the insulation can prevent vapor from making a pass through the insulation and how it can remain in it.

- Cost: This is another very consequential factor to consider. Usually, fixing insulation within your container will require handling costs relating to those whose services you would hire and the money you'd spend to get the necessary equipment. The only time this area gets good is when you have the technical know-how that will enable you to make the fixes yourself.

- Friendliness to the environment: Although this may not seem as much, your insulating material posing no harm to the environment is one thing you should look forward to enduring. The insulating materials, if eco-friendly, will help you enjoy living in your containers even more.

Types of Container Insulation

There are different kinds of container insulation, and here, we will discuss a few of them. One thing you should look out for while studying the kinds of insulation available should be the differences between them and how they can make your containers better insulators. Below are some properties about each type of container insulation.

Non-Traditional

1. This type of insulation is not too modern.
2. Most people would go for this kind of insulation because of their eco-friendliness.
3. This insulation is also one of the cheapest you can lay your hands on.
4. They have a low R-value and might not really be good options for most containers.
5. They work better for areas with a not too bad climate, i.e., where the temperature changes are within a bracket.
6. This insulation can only be done outside of the container with straw bale or hempcrete.

Hempcrete is almost like straw bale, but then the difference is that hempcrete is made out of a material with not too much strength.

Blanket

1. This kind of insulation comes in the form of lengths that have been previously cut to fill the height of your container walls.
2. The pieces of the blanket insulating material must be cut accurately.
3. This kind of insulation is somewhat fluffy and compressible.
4. It cannot support itself.
5. It has the nature of a blanket, except that it is thicker and constructed out of a material that is definitely not wool.
6. It is basically a mash of fibers that are stacked into small closures.
7. It is cheap to fix.
8. All you need to fix the studs of a blanket insulator is a stapler.
9. There are different forms of blanket insulation, and they are;

- Fiberglass insulation: This kind is made from recycled glass that is consequently woven into thin fibers. It is very common in Western countries.
- Slag wool insulation: This kind of insulation is made from slag, a waste product from the production of metals.
- Sheep wool insulation: This kind of insulation is made from the wool of sheep.
- Cotton insulation: This kind of insulation is made from cotton. This particular one is more expensive than the others and is of reused components

10. It allows the passage of water vapor.
11. Some of the materials used for constructing the blanket insulation could be sources of irritation to the eyes and skin.
12. Ensure that you use goggles and gloves while handling a blanket insulator.

Loose-Fill

1. This involves adding very small bits of insulating materials into the cavity between the inner and outer walls.

2. It comes in different forms, which include
   - Cellulose insulation: This insulation is offered from reused paper products that have been narrowly shredded into bits.
   - Loose-fill Fiberglass insulation: This kind of insulation is very identical to the fiberglass insulating material, but usually, it comes out ass less dense. This low density enables it to be easily moved by the machine.
   - Perlite insulation: This is a kind of insulation made by heated minerals that have gone through a series of expansions to become something very similar to foam pellets.
3. They allow the passage of vapor, so they aren't really the best choices for containers.

Expanded Form

1. This kind of insulation is usually produced in large boards and panels sized for particular wall heights.
2. They can support themselves.
3. You can make holes for the doors and windows in your container just by cutting through them.

4. When in expanded form, the gas could cause a reduction in the value of R when it is out of its confines.
5. This insulation is one that you can easily construct yourself.
6. There are different forms of expanded form insulators, and they include;
    - Open Cell Polyurethane Foam: This kind of insulation doesn't come out dense enough and usually would give the container a low R-value.
    - Closed Cell Polyurethane Foam: This insulation will help fill the small cells with a gas other than air that has great properties tied to heat conduction.
    - Extruded Polystyrene Foam: This insulation is made of small beads of a plastic nature that can be packed together into a closed-cell.
    - Expanded Polystyrene Foam: This kind of insulation starts off in a molten state.

Spray
1. This kind of insulation is one that can be fixed by applying a liquid mix that can consequently be hardened to form a solid.
2. This kind of insulation has the power to move into every nook and cranny of the container.
3. It works in a way that resists the movement of air particles.
4. The forms of spray insulation available include;
   - Open-cell spray polyurethane foam: This kind of spray insulation has a low R-value per inch as it allows the movement of air between the cells.
   - Closed-cell spray polyurethane: This is the commonest form of spray insulation. It has one of the largest R-values per inch and with no vapor transport. Over the years, though, the gas could leak out and end up with a lower R-value.

A Short message from the Author:

Hey, I hope you are enjoying the book? I would love to hear your thoughts!

Many readers do not know how hard reviews are to come by and how much they help an author.

```
Customer Reviews
★★★★★ 2
5.0 out of 5 stars ▾

5 star  ████████  100%    Share your thoughts with other customers
4 star                0%
3 star                0%    ┌─────────────────────────┐
2 star                0%    │  Write a customer review │  ⬅
1 star                0%    └─────────────────────────┘

See all verified purchase reviews ›
```

I would be incredibly grateful if you could take just 60 seconds to write a short review on Amazon, even if it is a few sentences!

\>> Click here to leave a quick review

Thanks for the time taken to share your thoughts!

Chapter 7

Receiving and Installing The Container

The hassle of having your shipping container loaded and delivered to you can stress anyone out. Since most people lack the necessary means to have their containers transported and installed, they hire third-party services. So, we will help you figure out how to go through with this stage and what it all entails.

Distance-Based Delivery Charges

When moving your shipping container, you will at every point in time need to evaluate the distance it will be traveling through. The farther it is from where you are, the more equipment you might need to get it to wherever you are. The distance here usually also has a direct proportion to the total amount of money you will spend.

Locally Sourced

This covers the deliveries made within a local environment, i.e., within your compound or across some areas within where you live. Sometimes, you could decide to move your container yourself, and indeed, if you have the right set of equipment at hand, that would not be a problem. The most important thing at the end of the day is that you get to save a whole lot of money. However, for containers with pounds well over five thousand, you might really need to employ some people to help you out. Usually, the cost incurred for locally sourced deliveries or container placements would fall within a bracket of a thousand dollars. The job should be done in less than an hour too. If you are moving your container from one place to another within your city, you definitely are going to need a trailer that could help you transport the container. Usually, the cost would fall within a bracket of one to four dollars per mile. The time for this delivery all depends on the presence or absence of traffic.

Internationally Sourced

Here, you get to move your container across thousands and millions of miles. Most of the companies set locally would not help with the movement of containers across countries. And that is because their drivers are unavailable for a time too long, and at the end of the day, they spend their profit all on the fueling of the trailer. So, you might want to go for a professional delivery company that can move containers to a place hundred miles away. Usually, they have other containers to carry, and that can help the drivers not return empty. That way, they can make maximum profit. Some of these professional companies include;

1. https://www.uship.com/: This is a delivery service provider that will help fetch you a listing for the shipment of your container.
2. Local Hauler: This delivery service will cause some of the local trucks in your area to provide a bid on the moving of your containers.
3. Freight agent: This company makes use of a mixture of connections from online boards and various industries.

Usually, for international deliveries of your container, you should spend an amount roughly close to one to four dollars per mile traveled. The time the whole process takes too depends on how congested the roads are. However, if you are moving your container around continents, you might need to work with two trucks. It usually requires you to spend a lot of money, but you definitely would get all the professional help you need. The cost of international deliveries usually cannot be placed, but then, you can obtain a rough estimate by adding the delivery cost in the country the truck left from and the one it arrives in. Other factors like shipping costs can also be added using a freight calculator. As regards the time, you need to know that distances traveled over the sea could take as long as a whole month to get over. So, you could prepare for a time roughly in between two weeks and a few months.

Finding Companies to Ship Your Containers

You can easily find shipping companies from the internet by typing in the necessary keywords, for example, "companies that ship containers." Usually, some companies deal with local deliveries, and some deal with international deliveries. So, ensure that you are very specific while searching and ensure you conduct thorough reviews of any company that piques your interest before going with them.

Length of Time of Delivery

The length of time it takes for your container to be delivered usually goes from about two weeks to a couple of months if it is done via sea. For local deliveries, you might get your containers delivered in a lesser time.

Siting and Offloading Your Shipping Containers

There are different methods through which you can offload and load your containers. The most typical method is still the tilt bed trailer method that involves the trailer sliding it off its bed.

1. Tilt-Bed Slide Off
   - It is the most standard way to offload a container off the back of a trailer.
   - The vehicle usually has a bed that can be tilted by the operation of a water-activated tilt bed. Once the bed inclines at the proper angle, the container slides off to the ground.
   - Once the end touches the ground, the driver moves the trailer forward a bit to allow the base to settle totally on the floor.
   - When using this method, you want to bear in mind the ground surface, overhead clearance, front clearance, and vertical stacking.
2. Side Loader
   - This side loader is fixed to a truck.
   - This way, your truck can offload just right at the area the foundation is in. Then, your container can also be offloaded just by the side.

- Here too, you might want to bear in mind factors like the ground surface, the overhead clearance, the vertical stacking, etc.
3. Forklift
    - The forklift is an equipment that is capable of carrying your container.
    - You can bring the forklift to your site by following the piggyback method, which is a method in which the forklift is fixed to the back of a trailer with forks.
    - The forklift may have to be transported to the site through a separate vehicle if you are using a separately trucked method.
    - When using a forklift, you might want to consider factors like the ground surface, the overhead clearance, the weight, and the vertical stacking.

Chapter 8

Installing The Utilities

Utilities are the fundamental requirements you should have in your container house, and they are discussed below.

Electricity

This is one of the most important factors that must be present in your container home. To get to use electricity, all you need to do is reach out to the electrical company in your area to help you make the necessary connections. The process of installation gets better when you have power lines close to the structure. The cost that could be incurred here depends on the distance between the power line and the container. You might also have to consider an overhead or underground electricity connection. You could opt for a temporary source of electricity until you are fully settled in your container home. Some examples of these temporary sources include generators and turbines.

Gas

This particular utility will help you heat up your stove and water. If your container is in an urban area, you'd easily get access to gas. In rural areas, you may need to buy a cylinder that helps you store the gas in volumes that will last for months.

Sewer and Septic

If your container is close to sewer sites, all you need to do is know how much it costs to get connected. This option is usually for those in the outskirts of the country. You could also fix a septic system in your container. This technique can be carried out at very low costs. The septic tanks are usually fixed beneath the ground.

Telecommunications

For containers located in areas where there are many hustles, i.e., the city, communications can be made via cables, television, and the internet. For places in the outskirt, the choices include satellites and DSL connects. If you have many options to choose from, you could go around and ascertain the prices. Then, go for the cheapest of the options.

Water

Water is another very important utility. You could plan on getting bottled water bottles, jars, or some other source of water supply. If you end up getting no option, you could bore a well beside your container home. You could also have water delivered regularly to you at a cost.

Chapter 9

Roofing The Container

Getting a roof for your container home is something that you could choose to do or not do, depending on your style and whether you have the money for it. However, when you roof your container, you end up saving yourself from several issues like energy bills and heat. Usually, with a roof, most of the heat that sits in your home could end up being lost by processes like convection.

Types of Roofing Styles

There are different kinds of roof styles that you could choose to use for your container, and they include the following;

Shed

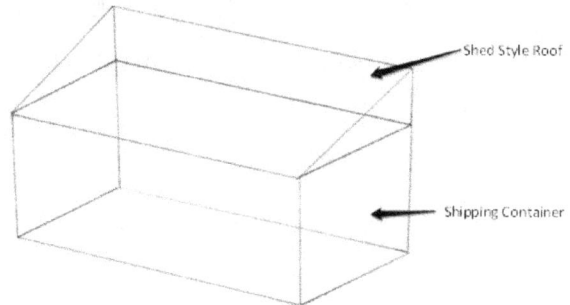

- This roof has a sloppy surface.
- It is very cheap to construct
- It can be easily built
- You can install this roof in a short period of time.
- The roof is one that works best if you plan on fixing solar panels for them.
- To fix this roof, follow the instructions below;
    - Weld right-angled plates across the length of the container roof.
    - Fix a wooden beam onto steel plates.
    - Screw-in the beams
    - Use steel bars to support the structure.
    - Use galvanized metal sheets to cover your roof.

- Make sure that your roof can be easily ventilated. For this, ensure that the soffit board has a gap of about an inch in the middle of it. This gap can be covered with wire mesh.

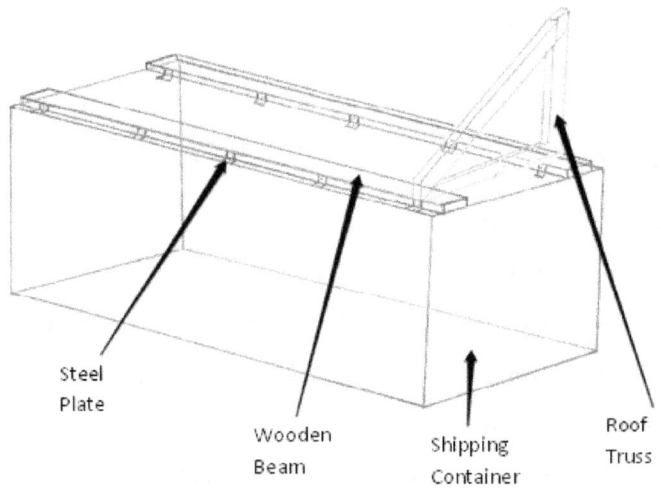

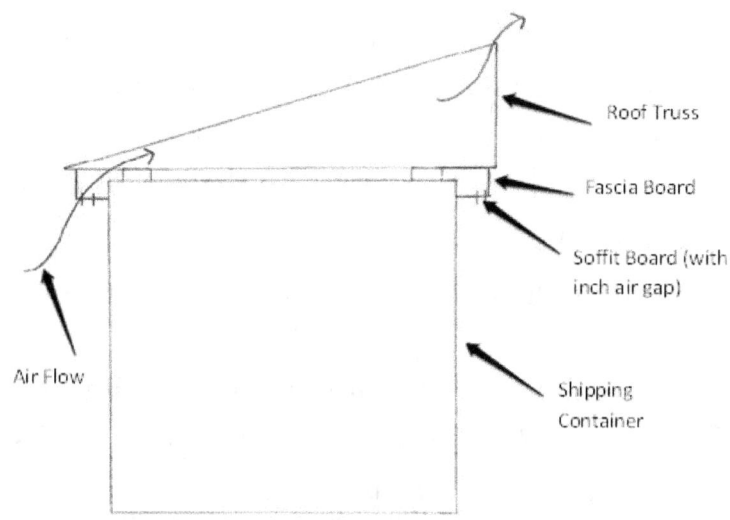

Gable

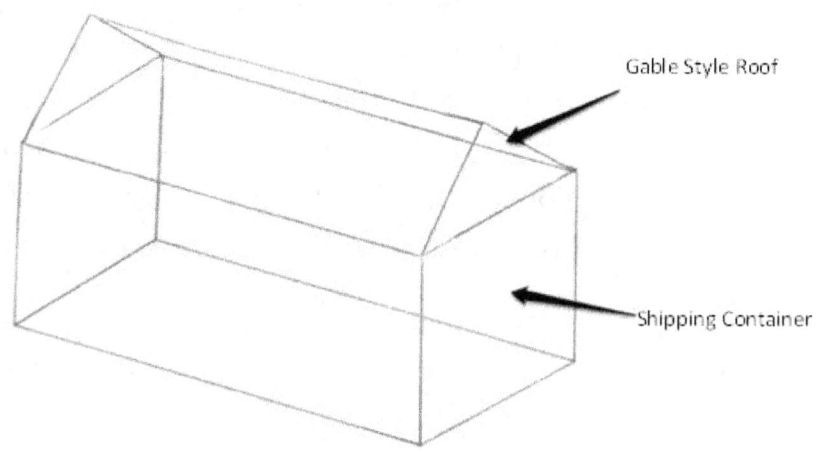

- It has a traditional and triangular outlook.
- It has a roof with a slope that helps to drain water easily.
- With this kind of roof, you are less likely to face leak issues.
- It offers more space for a ceiling than other kinds of roofs.
- To install the roof, follow the instructions below;
    o Weld a right-angled plate across the length of the container.
    o Fix a wooden beam to the plates
    o Screw-in the trusses to the plates.
    o Fix the purlins across the trusses to finish the structure.
    o To ensure that the roof is well ventilated, ensure that the trusses overhang, just like it is shown below. You could also fix a fascia and a soffit board underneath these trusses.

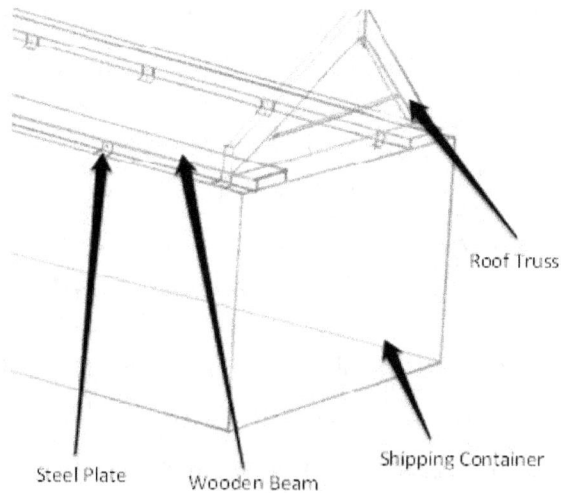

Flat

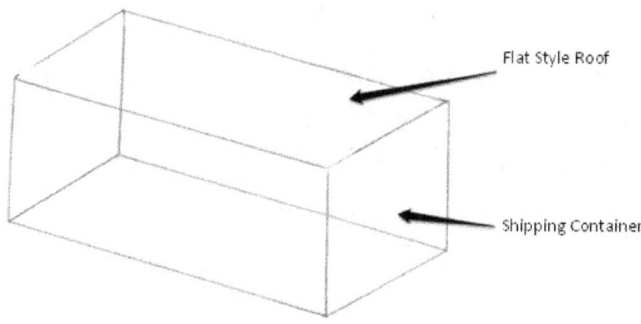

- This one is the roof the container originally has, and that could just be enough.
- The issue here is water stored up in the roof.

- You could lay a tarpaulin sheet on this kind of roof to protect it from rust and moisture.

Why You Need a Structural Engineer?

Having a structural engineer when building your roof will go a long way to help you because they would be able to help you make some necessary calculations like;

1. The dead load: This is the weight of all the materials you use to build your roof.
2. The live load: This is the weight of the equipment and the people that install the roof.
3. The transient load: This refers to a load of factors like rain, snow, and wind.

The amount of load your roof can carry is the amount of load it can bear before giving in. So, you must get someone who can help you make the right estimates so that you don't lose your roof.

Chapter 10

Flooring The Container

Flooring your container could become important when the floor has many dangerous and toxic chemicals that probably spilled on it during its former use. So, what are the things you can do to get rid of this issue?

Checking The Original Floors of The Container

You would notice that the floors of your container were initially built as an adaptation to life on the sea. So, you would usually find very thick hardwood floors constructed from birchwood or some other long-lasting wood. Birchwood is resistant to salty waters. So, first, ensure that you check the floors for signs of chemicals. You would often notice almost immediately since they usually leave the container with a choking or almost choking smell. You could also find out the kinds of chemicals used on the floor on the container's plate. There, you would also find details like the treatment and the name of the chemicals.

Should I Remove The Original Floor or Not?

Removing the original floor depends on the degree of toxicity of the chemicals used. Sometimes, especially when you buy used containers, you wouldn't be too sure that the floor wasn't previously damaged or replaced. You also wouldn't know what kind of chemicals had fused their way into the wood. Because of these uncertainties, you could choose to change the floors.

How to Remove The Original Floor?

To remove the original floors, all you mostly have to do is cut out the floor's bolts with a hand saw. The bolts are usually fixated by the cross parts and at a spacing of about ten inches. Once you have the bolts cut out, use a pry bar to push the wooden panels upward; this process is usually time-consuming.

Replacing a Container Floor

To replace the floors of your shipping containers, you would find several replacement options out there. Such options include the following, but then, take note that the options listed here are not all but are the more popular options available out there.

Best Flooring For Flatpack Containers
1. Bamboo flooring: This kind of floor comes out as one that is very cheap, durable, and flexible. You don't need to do anything to this kind of floor before fixing them in your container.
2. Carpet flooring: This technique involves you using a carpet to cover the original plywood floor.
3. Steel flooring: This is a kind of flooring that is will provide you with durable and water-resistant floors.
4. Vinyl flooring: This kind of floor involves the use of vinyl. It helps you see that your container is maintainable.
5. Linoleum flooring: This kind of floor is the kind you would use when making an environment-friendly replacement. It is resistant to bacteria and very biodegradable. They usually would last for a time as long as forty years.

Chapter 11

Building A Wall Inside The Container

Like homes, shipping containers can be divided into compartments lined with brick boundaries and other walls. The walls are usually protected by insulators, though. Here, we will discuss a few ways by which you can construct a wall in your container home.

Framing

Framing is a technique that professionals usually orchestrate, and that is because it utilizes essential and intrinsic factors like wires, insulation, etc.

- Start framing by adding corrugation fixes. You could start the procedure either vertically or horizontally before using spray to plaster the sheets completely.
- The fixes will help to get rid of unnecessary gaps in your container home, so once you fix them in, you can go ahead to work with the framing materials.
- Once you fix the inserts, you can fix the panels to the outer edges of the container.

- You could skip the process with frames and insulate the panels right onto the outer surface of the steel. This technique will consequently fetch you more holes in your container.

Framing Materials

1. Steel Strips
   - They are used for welding the sides of a frame.
   - They are great for tropical climate areas.
2. Wood Posts

   - They have a dimension of two inches by two inches.
   - They can be fixed with tiny nails.
3. Aluminum Strips

- They are made by joining thin metallic strips.
- The strips are usually very simple to fix.

Insulation

Once you are done fixing frames, the next thing you'd want to do is get the container insulated. A shipping container must have the right amount of insulation. These insulators will help you control changes in weather conditions. To know the type of insulation available for you as a container homeowner, you can refer to the already discussed types of insulation in Chapter 6.

Wall-Paneling

When you are done with the insulation, the next thing to do is cover the wall so that you have no space in between. Here, there are no seams required. All you need to do is paint and polish.

Types of Container Interior Walls
1. Drywall
    - It is the commonest wall used.
    - It has complete paneling.
    - It has a traditional finish
    - The seams are totally covered
    - It moves, and so, it's prone to cracks.
2. Plywood
    - It has a rough finish.
    - It is good for use in a shop with plenty of tools.
    - It has very obvious paneling.
3. Fiberglass Reinforced Panels
    - The seams are hidden with trim strips.
    - They are resistant to water.
    - They can be washed.
4. Sandalwood
    - It has an interior wall that is wonderful for the living room.
    - It has an invisible grain.
    - The seams are hidden with polished strips.
    - They look very smooth and regular.
    - They don't suffer any damages from being mobile.

5. Aluminum Sheets
    - They are used for the outer surfaces of a shipping container.
    - They are insulated by foams a little bit.
    - They have a sleek coat.
    - They have easy-to-see seams.
    - The sheets are easy to clean.
    - They can easily be transferred from one place to the other.

Chapter 12

Installing The Doors and Windows

Doors and windows in your container home come as fundamental needs that your containers cant do without. Let's explore what this section entails a little deeper.

1. Choose the door, window, and frame: You will notice that doors and windows can be structured out of different materials, and these factors usually affect how they are fixed. Shipping containers are usually made out of steel, so you should try to use a material that would not negatively affect the steel. For example, when aluminum comes in contact with steel, it ends up rusting due to a process known as galvanic corrosion. If you choose to work with wood, steel, or something else that is not metallic, you could end up not having to bother about corrosion.

2. Choose the size of the tube that you'd use for the frame of the box section: It would be best to have

an architect help you calculate the size of the angle that would be used for framing the doors and windows. To get the correct angle, you might need to consider the load you place at the opening and the depth of the finished wall. The size of the frame is usually obtained by using a steel square or steel angle.

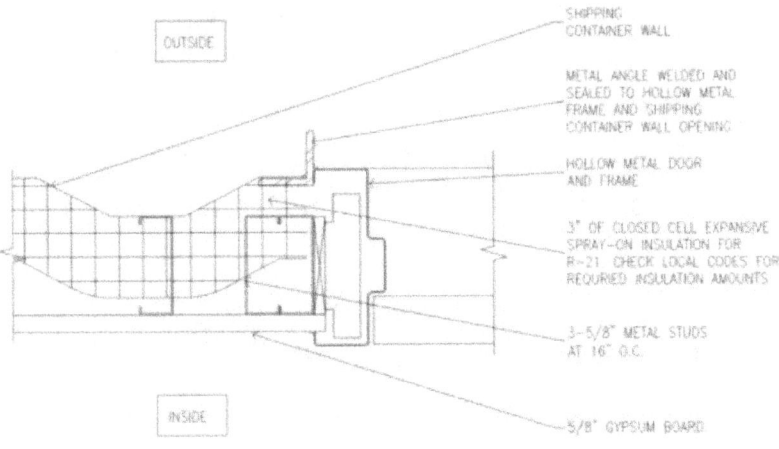

METAL ANGLE FRAMED OPENING
FOR DOOR INSTALLATION
JAMB DETAIL (HEAD SIMILAR)

3. Cut and join the box section frame together: This is where you can measure the exact size of the box section. You could also determine the angle in which the frame would exist in. The measurements you made inside have to be pretty

much close to the values you get for the outer measurements. Any extra space can be covered with a sealant. Most of the door frames do not have a bottom, so you may need to cut out supports between the vertical legs that are at the end of the box frame.

4. Mark the areas where the door and window are to be attached to the container wall: To make this step easy, join two quarter-inch-thick steel supports of three by four inches to the end of the shipping container. These supports should be at the place where the box section is to be fixed. The plates usually would hold up the box section frame that is to be traced. After doing that, you can use a piece of chalk to draw the cut line around the box's frame. For the box frame, ensure that the mark is not any greater than 1/16" from the projection box. Finally, remove the two temporary metal support plates and then smoothen the rest of the surfaces.

5. Work with a hand grinder to cut the door and window holes: You can start by cutting the

bottom and then proceeding to the sides. When you finish cutting along the bottom and sides, you can fix two of a two by a four-inch window into the space. Ensure that the bottom of the windows have their tops touching the uppermost inner layers of the shipping container. Ensure you enforce as many safety measures as possible.

6. Weld the angle frame into the walls of the container.: Before you begin to weld the metal frame to shipping containers, ensure that the walls are not bending towards any angle. If it has, you might need to fix some hooks to it so as to pull it back into place. You could also make use of a metal hardener at the bow to get rid of the dent. To start with, use tack welds to attach the frame to the container. Then, you can proceed to fix a full weld across the frame's uppermost edges. Next, fix the welds that are about four inches long to each side of the frame. Then, go on to weld the one-inch stitch at the ten-inch center.

7. Fix the door or window within the box or angle section frame: Since aluminum doors or frames,

when attached to steel box frames, can cause galvanic corrosion, you could opt for materials like neoprene, plastic dividers, etc., to separate the different materials. The painted surface will also go a long way in reducing corrosion. Always ensure that the holes left by the screws are without paint. Some other connectors like stainless steel screws also do not cause corrosion. So, in all, you end up not cutting extra holes into the frame or cause something ugly like water infiltration.

8. Seal the joints around the door or window: Of course, you'd find spaces in the work. So, you will have to seal them with sealants that complement the beauty of your house. To hide the sealing works, all you have to do is paint the frame and walls with the sealants.

9. Fix finishes to the edges of the side and window: The finishes done interiorly are usually in line with the window frame. The interior wall location will help you determine how deep the section of your box can be. For exterior finishes like stucco,

you obviously would need to fix flashing between the outer edge and the outer finishes. Ensure that you do not allow for water molecules to form within the nooks.
10. Safety precautions to take when fixing a door or window: Always ensure that you do not work alone because you'd be dealing with heavy and sharp metals. Besides, the work will come out even faster when you work with others.

Chapter 13

Fixing The Exterior of The Container

The exterior of your container is what is defined as the true aesthetics of your container home. With the right design implementation and adequate styling, you can be sure that you can get your house to resemble one of the beautiful houses of the twenty-first century. The beauty of your container also depends on the materials you utilize for the construction of the exterior walls. Sometimes, the items of nature, such as the trees and flowers, could also add to the outlook, giving it the most charming impressions.

Cladding Materials

Cladding materials are very many out there, but you will only find a few of them that can be used for containers. Since the walls of a container home are not breathable, you have to ensure that you use an outer cladding to allow the influx of air. This technique is so that the moisture that peradventure gets in through the pores can be allowed the freedom to leave. If the moisture remains trapped, usually, what happens is that the structure gets destroyed due to the build-up of moisture. It could also cause wooden supports to undergo rots. The following characteristics determine the kind of cladding material you go for;

- The color of your container house
- The type of finish you employ for your container house.
- The cost of the materials that you employ for the construction of your container house.
- The R-factor.

Timber

Timber is one material from which you can obtain wooden logs. When these wooden logs are used in beautifying your container homes, you get something that looks as striking as anything. It is one material that gives the medieval feel, and it only gets better when you coat the surface of the timber with natural colors. The most commonly used wood includes the Canadian Western Red Cedar and the Redwood. The other sets of hardwood include chestnut and oakwood. Even without them being treated, these wood types can still come out as one of the best by resisting moisture and the effect of decaying organisms. You could also get them in colors like gold, red, and grey.

Timber exists in different forms, and they include clapboards, shingles, and half-logs which you can utilize when employing the overlapping and joining technique. To fix timber logs in your container home, you need not have too much technical know-how. Just by selectively interlocking wooden pieces for aesthetic purposes, you can easily get what you want.

Bamboo

Bamboo is one tree that grows very quickly, so, you using them to decorate the exterior of your container home could come out as one of the best decisions you could ever make. They are usually used to decorate your wood as they exist in the form of tubular stems. When they are exposed to high humidity, you usually will find out that they can stand the test of time. The only issue you could experience with them is that they could lose their natural hues and have mildew growing across their lengths. So, to prevent the time the fading actually occurs, the stems are usually coated. Bamboo stems are usually cut open along their lengths, after which the outermost layers are peeled off to ensure that their natural hue is kept.

Engineered Wood

This wood merges the natural outlook of natural wood and the durability of synthetic materials. They are also known as the Wood-Plastic Composites. They are composed of about fifty percent of powdered wood fibers and about forty-five percent of high-density polyethylene. The high-density polyethylene is a non-toxic constituent that is employed in the food industry.

They aren't receptive to factors like mildew, mold, or rot. They also offer a lot of resistance to ultraviolet rays and thermal effects. This wood exists in various colors, and it usually is all about choosing whichever suits you. Engineered wood, unfortunately, cannot be stained, so the moment you fix them, you can't really change its colors.

Fiber-Cement Boards

These boards are made from a mix of concrete and some other substances like fillers and pigments. Usually, concrete is found in higher percentages in the boards, and the fibers are used to support the concrete by a factor of about ten percent. You could also add concrete circles of alumina that will help fetch you a final product that is rigid and unchanging. Since fiber-cement boards are constructed from natural sources, you'd find out that they are resistant to ultraviolet rays, rots, and fire. They can also be found in several shapes and colors. These boards usually are available colored, but then, you could repaint them if you desire.

Composite Materials

These are mixtures of two or more materials that help to provide a product that is way better than each of the other constituents. There are several reasons why you'd want to try out composite materials for the outdoors, and they include the following characteristics;

1. Strength
2. Lightweight

3. Moisture-resistance
4. UV-ray resistance
5. Low-temperature resistance.
6. Resistance to insect attack
7. Resistance to discoloring.

Even though they may be purchased at a fairly high price, composite materials come out as very elegant and durable. They are also non-biodegradable. Engineered wood is usually seen as one of the many composite materials available.

Composite Panels

These panels exist as layers of insulation between metallic sheets. The sheets usually are made of Aluminum or steel. This feature gives them the name, 'sandwich.' They come out as a principal component of cladding and help to insulate your container home. If you plan to construct walls that will bear a lot of weight, it is best to use composite panels for the job. The composite panels have folded metallic sheets on the outer surface. They have a metal finish and are resistant to factors like moisture, mold, mildew, insects, and rots. Their initial colors usually do not fade with time.

Metal

Fixing a sheet of metal onto another sheet may not make too much of a sense, but then, it offers a lot of good treats. It is not affected by insects, ultraviolet rays, or even fire. You can clean the surfaces or have them repainted if some color fading occurs. Metallic claddings are made from metals like aluminum, copper, brass, stainless steel, and so on. Those made of copper alloys are usually more costly.

Cladding Installation

Cladding can be fixed on the outer surface of your container with the aid of a pressboard that helps to stake the installments with nails. You could also use metallic screws, but it usually would take a lot of time and energy to fix. Besides, having the cladding filled with holes can reduce the impermeability of the container home.

Cladding Only

This is a technique you might want to consider if you are more bothered about the aesthetic look of your container house. Ensure that in all, you leave a bit of a gap between the structural walls and the outer cladding. This way, you can help to prevent situations related to the overheating of your container home. For this, you would need wooden support that is clamped down with glue. Take note that you wouldn't want to limit the container's structural integrity any less than normal.

Cladding With Exterior Insulation

Fusing exterior insulating materials could be a complicated process, as you would not want a situation where there's a layer of air molecules or gases between the insulation and the walls of the container. This could cause the container to degrade progressively when it is exposed to moisture.

Painting The Container

Painting your container will help you beautify your house even more as it adds a luster to the original mundane color of your container home. When a professional oversees the painting process, he will ensure the paint job comes out great and lasts a long time. Professionals know how to prep the container to get a smooth surface they can paint on, and they are also knowledgeable on the right products to use.

The kind of paint to be used?

For the best possible outcome, containers should be painted with primer paint and an exterior premium paint in one, both of which come in satin or flat finish. On the other hand, a separate primer can be applied and then a topcoat. Two coats of paint are most times enough to ensure it lasts, but you may require more depending on your choice of color and the needed coverage. Also, you can apply insulation coatings on the top paint to prevent and deflect heat and anti-corrosion coatings; this helps to add strength to the rusted or corroded areas of the container.

Several colors of paints are available that can be chosen for your container, but then note that when making your selection,

- Lighter colors will need extra coats of paint for the right coverage to be gotten. Light colors will also display marks or dirt much easier.

- Darker colors may cause the container's interior to be hotter in summer, but they better mask imperfections than lighter colors.

- Use colors that blend nicely with your ambient environment.

When you use the right kind of paint, the lifespan of your shipping container can be prolonged and made to look brand new.

Chapter 14

Interior Design Ideas

This section will discuss a few design ideas that you can explore to make your container home look exquisite to live in and help with space management.

Design Idea 1—Sliding doors

This technique does not involve dead spaces. Dead spaces are areas that you cannot use because of the perimeter the actual doors will pass through when you open them. For example, a thirty-two-inch-wide door will open by sweeping over about eleven square feet of the area, and that is indeed a lot of wasted space. Sliding doors will only open when you move them in straight lines, so that still comes out as a better choice. Let's take a look t a few of these doors.

Barn Doors

Barn doors are doors made out of rustic wood to give the feel of actual barns. They usually are there to add beauty to the room. The only issue about these doors is that the bolt that holds the door down is usually fixed to the wall. So, when the door is open, it covers a large portion of the wall.

Pocket Doors

Pocket doors are much similar to barn doors, but the only issue is that the door has to go into a compartment when it is opened. In cases where a thick portion of the wall is not available, this option may not come out as very feasible. The walls' surfaces on both sides of this floor could work well as surfaces for shelves and some other furniture.

Design Idea 2—Convertible Couches

Convertible couches are couches that can be turned into beds. There are different types available, and each one offers a lot of flexibility to the design plan of your house. A convertible couch will take less space than a full-sized bed in your bedroom and could intermittently be used as a sitting area.

Futon

The Futon bed was sourced from the Japanese, and it is a mattress that can fold across its length, and when you place it on a frame, you get a sofa. They can also be folded into an L-shape.

Daybed

Daybeds utilize a regular mattress and a headboard that goes right to the bed's long side. The sideboard is usually formed when the backrest is used as a couch. The narrow twin-sized mattress can also be used here.

Foldout Couch/Sleeper Sofa Chaise

This kind of sofa has the look of a traditional couch only that when you get rid of the cushions, you see a folded mattress and a frame that can be folded following a Transformer technique. The cushion you sleep on here is usually different from what you sit on.

Design Idea 3 — Using The Walls

Here, you get to make good use of the walls. This way, you end up getting more floor space to yourself.

Wall-Mounted Desks

This desk is practically suspended in the air. It is usually fixed tightly to the wall, and most times, it does not need extra supports from the floor. It has a large surface you can use for working and can be folded against the wall when you don't need it. It is usually supported with chains from above.

Tv Mounts

Another way by which you can effectively save space is by mounting your TV to the wall so that you don't have to get a separate Tv stand or table. You can position the Tv in any direction too, and so, usually, you'd be able to watch your Tv even from the kitchen.

Wall-Mounted Fans

The wall-mounted fans are used to get air flowing around the container. All you have to do is mount the container to the wall and then have the fan built inside the container.

Design Idea 4—Rooms Without Walls

This technique allows you to have much more space than you can imagine. The only issue is that you might not be able to get enough privacy to yourself.

Hanging Fabric Curtains

This step involves you making use of curtains sewn out of clothes. A dark and heavy fabric will help you prevent light waves completely, but a thin material will allow in a lot of light and sound.

Hanging Beaded Curtains

This technique allows you to make use of vertical dividers that have beads attached to their length. This way, more light waves and sound can actually find their way through. You could make things more beautiful by using beads of different sizes and colors.

Folding Panel Dividers

A folding panel divider comes in different forms, and they include one that can be folded in three places. While working with this, go for designs and textures that blend with the décor of your container.

Rotating Entertainment Center

This is one technique in which a Tv and the rest of the media are placed on a surface that can spin through an angle of 180-degrees. Sometimes, it could spin through a greater angle, and other times, it could spin just through a narrower section. The whole point is that you can keep the center region free and then walk around without many borders.

Double-Sided Fireplace

This technique is excellent for areas with icy climatic conditions. It can be a great source of warmth for two areas of your container home.

Chapter 15

Shipping Container Home FAQs

Here, we will look at a couple of questions that other people have had to ask regarding their container homes. Hopefully, it would help you make the right choices as you venture into building your container home while avoiding making costly mistakes.

1. What is the difference between a container house and a regular tiny house?

    You would find out that container houses and the other small houses are the kinds that you will find in more places today. And even though they offer a lot of comfort to the owner, they both still have their respective differences.

    Here, we will evaluate a few of these differences.

    - Space: Your container house does not necessarily have to be tiny. You could make it bigger by adjoining two, three, or even more containers. However, a tiny house, even though designed specially, cannot be extended. A standard tiny home has dimensions of about nine inches by twenty-three inches, and usually, it could be larger, depending on the size of your budget. But then, a container is about twenty feet to forty feet long and can be made bigger by joining several containers together.

- Cost: The money you would spend building a tiny house should be about forty thousand dollars. How much more you spend depends hugely on the designs you integrate with your plans. A single shipping container sells for about two thousand five hundred dollars, and you might also want to add the cost that can be incurred on the design, transport, delivery, labor, and so much more.
- Sustainability: The level of sustainability of a tiny home and a shipping container will provide you depend largely on the materials you use in constructing them. A smaller space will require only a few materials, while a bigger one would require more energy costs.
- Renovation: Both tiny homes and container homes have advantages and disadvantages as

regards this very factor. A container home can always be extended, but then, it means that you can easily work with a size that is good for the size of your family. However, factors like the roof and insulation only make the process a bit more complicated. Container homes could also suffer issues like rust and damage by chemicals. Dealing with this issue could be very demanding, but then, if carefully treated, it could be worth your time and money. A container home can stand the test of time if properly managed. On the other hand, a tiny home cannot be expanded, but then, you get to make a lot of useful choices as regards the materials you use and your design.

2. How long can a shipping container last?

A shipping container will last for about twenty-five years or more if well maintained. All you just need to do is watch out for issues like rust. You could also help the structure by covering it with an outer layer, e.g., wood.

3. How much will I spend building a container house?

   The amount of money you spend building your container houses varies hugely. Most times, what is spent falls in the range of $1400 and $4000. Other factors like the age, condition, and the size of the container can also determine the amount of money you spend generally. Here, a few of the prices were listed;

   - For standard new shipping containers of a length of twenty feet, you might spend about $3100.
   - For twenty feet standard used shipping containers, you could spend about $2100.
   - For twenty feet high cube new shipping containers, you could spend about $3100.
   - For twenty feet high cube used shipping containers, you could spend about $2100.
   - For forty feet standard new shipping containers, you could spend about $5600.
   - For forty feet standard used shipping container, you could spend about $2850.

- For forty feet high cue new shipping container, you could spend about $5800.

The other factors that affect the total cost incurred in building a container home include

- Availability: You have to consider how available the container you plan on getting is. The ones that are far away may need that you spend more money and vice versa.
- Permit documents: This factor depends on the type of permits you need to settle before building your container home.
- Site: Building your container home on a site that is embedded with many rocks and tree stumps will require that you spend more money eradicating them.
- Delivery: The money you spend on this factor depends hugely on the distance the container travels.

4. Are shipping containers water-proof?

They are not water-proof, but they offer a bit of resistance to water, which means that they can resist water to a large extent. So, things like rain and snow can easily be prevented from finding their way into your home.

5. Are shipping containers safe to live in?

If you are buying the container from the manufacturer, you can be sure that the container is safe for residential purposes. All you just have to do is inform the producers that you want the floors to be free from toxic chemicals and paint. However, there could be the slightest possibility that the container has been treated with chemicals for used shipping containers. To solve that issue, all you need to do is place a floor covering over the original floor and ensure that it is non-breathable.

6. Are shipping containers hurricane-proof?

Shipping containers were originally made for life on the sea to withstand pressure as high as hundred meters per hour. They get even safer and stronger when attached to foundations, and then they get to withstand more pressure.

7. Can I build a house under 50k?

Yes, it is possible to get a house that is within the fifty thousand bracket. Mostly, all this will require is you doing the majority of the hassle yourself. You will need to get the raw materials ready, and it all gets good when you order them directly from the companies that supply them.

8. How can I connect shipping container houses?

    One common way by which you can do this is by producing a seal with welded corner posts and thin metal sheets. Add a little bit of roofing cement, and you would be good to go. You might also need to fix rolled roof flashes outside and inside your container before using the roofing cement.

9. Which states allow shipping containers to be built?

    In the United States, almost all the states are receptive to container homes, such as Missouri, Massachusetts, Maryland, Minnesota, Michigan, and Maine. But then, ensure that you check first with your city and town before ordering for your container to ensure container homes are allowed to be constructed in your city.

The end... almost!

Hey! We've made it to the final chapter of this book, and I hope you've enjoyed it so far.

If you have not done so yet, I would be incredibly thankful if you could take just a minute to leave a quick review on Amazon

Reviews are not easy to come by, and as an independent author with a little marketing budget, I rely on you, my readers, to leave a short review on Amazon.

Even if it is just a sentence or two!

So if you really enjoyed this book, please...

>> Click here to leave a brief review on Amazon.

I truly appreciate your effort to leave your review, as it truly makes a huge difference.

Chapter 16

Shipping Container Home Mistakes To Avoid

Container homes are one of the best housing projects to execute. However, in constructing your container home, the possibility exists that you could get distracted and make a couple of mistakes that could cost you severly. Here we will study a few of the mistakes and then see how you can avoid making them.

1. Fixing your container on a weak foundation.

    Foundations, like the word implies, are the first things that should be constructed before any structure can be erected. Earlier in this book, the importance of foundations was discussed. So, what happens when you build on a weak foundation? Something about the ground is that it sinks with time. There could be a landslide or some other issue, and it gets worse when you have about two to three container homes merged together. That way, the container homes could end up getting pulled apart. You also should ensure that you construct your foundations out of strong components so that they can withstand the pressure of whatever you place in them. A good foundation works to spread the weight of the containers around the ground equally.

2. Making wrong estimates as regards your ship size.

The containers used for shipping are not usually the same as those you would use to construct your home. Both of them come in different sizes, so the high cube containers are there to add extra inches to the height of your house. Insulating your container home will cut out of this space, and usually, what you end up having is a reduction in the general space available.

3. Buying containers that are in bad condition.

As discussed earlier, you can buy different kinds of containers for your container home, but then, now is the time to consider the purpose they would be serving. Since you would be living in it, it has to be something of a quality that can stand the test of time. It has to be able to resist several factors like temperature, pressure, and weather conditions. Buying something that is already weak might need you to spend money on repairs later on. For example, containers meant for homes usually would have to be cut and welded at some point to construct doors and windows. All of these things work to reduce the structural integrity of the container. So, ensure that you properly scrutinize it before you get a container to prevent issues later on.

4. Paying no attention to codes and building regulations.

   Getting the right information is essential to avoid a scenario where your container home is dislodged from its original position. So, you have to ensure that you go through all the necessary permit laws of wherever you intend to put your container. Some countries, for example, are not too receptive to the whole container home idea, so you have to be careful. Not paying attention to codes and set-down laws could also lead to unnecessary time delays. So, ensure that you get the important information from whoever coordinates the zoning office of your area.

5. Using the wrong kind of insulation.

The type of climate that plays out in your area comes as a factor that hugely determines the kind of insulation that you use for your home. If you make the mistake of fixing the wrong insulation, you could suffer the risk of excessive heat or excessively cold temperatures inside your container. Some conditions like rain could cause the rusting of your container with time, and in a place where you have rainfall continuously over time, you could utilize insulation types like spray foam insulation. So, ensure that you make the right inquiries before working with any insulation.

6. Cutting out too much steel from the container.

A container can get really weak when you continuously cut out metal scraps from it. This way, your container could end up getting very weak, and consequently, it could lose its balance. So, what you should always look out for is a solid container home that can stand the effects of forces like wind. Even if you have to cut out steel scraps from your container, ensure that the cuts are made at a reasonable distance apart from each other. You could also try implementing steel beams into the structure of the container to support it.

7. Employing the services of an inexperienced or unprofessional home builder.

    This is one biggest mistake anyone can possibly make. So to ensure that your container home doesn't turn out bad, get someone who understands the technicalities of container construction and is very good at merging one or two things to get the desired effect. You have to ensure that the builder knows every important thing about every component, the uses, the types, the safe choices to make, and so on. The kind of work, the person, ends up rendering to you will largely depend on how much they know. So, to avoid a situation where you spend more than you originally planned for, ensure that you make the right inquiries before employing just anyone.

Conclusion

A container home is one of the best options anyone could ever make, and indeed, with the right amount of knowledge, you could create something exquisite, durable, and magnificent. Factors like insulation, foundation, flooring, compartmentalization, decoration, painting, and so on discussed in this book are all equally important. Suppose you have little or no experience in technically related things like house construction and decoration. In that case, you could hire someone with the relevant expertise and experience to help you out. And with that, you could have a container house so beautiful that it'd compete with an actual house.

With the pricey information shared in the pages of this book, I sure hope this book serves you a great deal as you venture into building your own container home.

I wish you all the best!

References

Roberts, T. (2021, February 20). *12 Tips You Need to Know Before Building a Shipping Container Home*. Rise. https://www.buildwithrise.com/stories/12-tips-you-need-to-know-before-building-a-shipping-container-home

Containers, D. (2021, June 2). *How to Choose the Right Shipping Containers*. Discover Containers. https://www.discovercontainers.com/complete-guide-to-buying-shipping-containers/

Containers, D. (2021, June 2). *How and Where to Buy Shipping Containers*. Discover Containers.

https://www.discovercontainers.com/how-to-purchase-your-shipping-containers/

Containers, D. (2021b, June 2). *How and Where to Buy Shipping Containers*. Discover Containers.

https://www.discovercontainers.com/how-to-purchase-your-shipping-containers/

Containers, D. (2021a, April 8). *Shipping Container Site Preparation*. Discover Containers.

https://www.discovercontainers.com/shipping-container-site-preparation/

Containers, D. (2020, October 1). *Shipping Container Home Foundations 101*. Discover Containers.

https://www.discovercontainers.com/shipping-container-home-foundation-types/

Okelo, A. (2021, May 25). *How to Build a Wall Inside a Shipping Container*. Dengarden. https://dengarden.com/misc/How-To-Build-A-Wall-Inside-A-Shipping-Container

Lane, L. (2021, May 24). *How Do You Put a Door and Window in a Shipping Container?* Live in a Container. https://liveinacontainer.com/how-do-you-put-a-door-and-window-in-a-shipping-container/

Home, C. I. (2020, May 26). *Container House – Exterior Finish*. IContainerHome.Com.

htttps://icontainerhome.com/container-house-exterior-finish/#google_vignette

www.ingramcontent.com/pod-product-compliance
Lightning Source LLC
Chambersburg PA
CBHW071418070526
44578CB00003B/599